# BAM!
## Boys Advocacy and Mentoring

**The Routledge Series on Counseling and Psychotherapy with Boys and Men**

SERIES EDITOR

Mark S. Kiselica
The College of New Jersey

ADVISORY BOARD

Deryl Bailey
University of Georgia

David Lisak
University of Massachusetts – Boston

Chris Blazina
University of Houston

William Liu
University of Iowa

J. Manuel Casas
University of California – Santa Barbara

James O'Neil
University of Connecticut

Matt Englar-Carlson
California State University - Fullerton

Steve Wester
University of Wisconsin – Milwaukee

Ann Fischer
Southern Illinois University – Carbondale

VOLUMES IN THIS SERIES

# BAM!
## Boys Advocacy and Mentoring

### A Leader's Guide to Facilitating Strengths-Based Groups for Boys

### Helping Boys Make Better Contact by Making Better Contact with Them

**PETER MORTOLA | HOWARD HITON | STEPHEN GRANT**

Routledge
Taylor & Francis Group
New York   London

Routledge
Taylor & Francis Group
270 Madison Avenue
New York, NY 10016

Routledge
Taylor & Francis Group
2 Park Square
Milton Park, Abingdon
Oxon OX14 4RN

© 2008 by Taylor & Francis Group, LLC
Routledge is an imprint of Taylor & Francis Group, an Informa business

Printed in the United States of America on acid-free paper
10 9 8 7 6 5 4 3 2 1

International Standard Book Number-13: 978-0-415-96318-3 (Softcover)

---

**Library of Congress Cataloging-in-Publication Data**

---

Mortola, Peter.
    BAM! boys advocacy and mentoring : a leader's guide to facilitating strengths-based groups for boys, helping boys make better contact by making better contact with them / Peter Mortola, Howard Hiton, and Stephen Grant.
        p. cm. --  (The Routledge series on counseling and psychotherapy with boys and men ; v. 2)
    Includes bibliographical references and index.
    ISBN 978-0-415-96318-3 (softcover)

1.  Boys--Psychology. 2.  Teenage boys--Psychology. 3.  Boys--Life skills guides. 4.  Teenage boys--Life skills guides. 5. Mentoring--United States--Handbooks, manuals, etc. 6.  Youth development--United States. 7.  Social work with youth--United States. I. Hiton, Howard. II. Grant, Stephen (Stephen T.) III. Title.
    HQ775.M727 2007

362.7--dc22

2007024860

Visit the Taylor & Francis Web site at
http://www.taylorandfrancis.com

and the Routledge Web site at
http://www.routledge.com

# Contents

# Series Editor's Foreword

Every once in a great while, a handful of dedicated mental health profession-als discover that they have a shared vision. Stephen Grant, Howard Hiton, and Peter Mortola enjoyed such a discovery after each of them, in their own, separate ways, had devoted much of their careers to helping boys. In his role as a consultant to several school districts in the Portland, Oregon, area, How-ard had been examining data related to academic achievement, and, in the process, he became acutely aware of the particular problems boys tended to have with their educational experiences. Meanwhile, Stephen was leading school-based counseling groups for boys and serving as an advocate for male students, and Peter was running a group for boys in a Portland elementary school and teaching a course on lifespan development at Lewis and Clark College, which had included extensive coverage of gender issues. A fourth professional, Lois Orner of Portland Impact, an organization providing men-tal health services to youths and families, was aware of the overlapping inter-ests of Howard, Stephen, and Peter, so she suggested to the three men that they consider getting together so that they could learn about what each other was doing. Fortunately for us, the three men heeded Lois's suggestion. They began to share their observations with one another about the developmental needs of boys and the difficult challenges they had encountered when trying to help boys in schools. As they tried to devise new ways to serve boys in a gender-sensitive manner, they realized that there was no curriculum espe-cially designed for doing enhancement groups with boys. They decided that both they and other professionals could benefit from a hands-on book that describes the difficulties boys experience and the process of helping young men through strategies that tap into the ways boys relate to the world. So, they poured their energy and their extensive knowledge and wisdom about boys into writing a manuscript that would be devoted to teaching others about how to facilitate strengths-based groups with school-aged boys. *BAM! Boys Advocacy and Mentoring: A Leader's Guide to Facilitating Strengths-Based Groups for Boys* is the wonderful product of that collaboration.

I am proud to introduce *BAM!* as the second volume in *The Routledge Series on Counseling and Psychotherapy with Boys and Men*. One of my goals as editor of this exciting new series is to develop the most comprehensive set of books on helping boys and men that has ever been assembled. Concern about the emotional lives of boys and men permeates our society and has created a tremendous need to understand the male socialization process and the hardships of boys and men, and how to utilize male ways of relating and male strengths during the helping process. Because *BAM!* addresses these issues by providing innovative and male-friendly group activities for boys, it is a perfect book to follow *Counseling Troubled Boys: A Guidebook for Practitioners*, which is the first book in the series.

I invite you to enjoy the marvelous work of Stephen Grant, Howard Hiton, and Peter Mortola and to keep your eyes open for future books in the series, which will be focused on many different special populations of boys and men whose concerns warrant our compassionate attention and assistance.

**Mark S. Kiselica, Editor**
*The Routledge Series on Counseling and Psychotherapy with Boys and Men*
*The College of New Jersey*
*May 18, 2007*

# BAM! Introduction

## About the Authors

BAM! POW! KABOOM! ZOOM! Boys burst forth into the world, into their families, schools, and social arenas with unique energy and needs. Understanding these needs and supporting boys' development has been the focus of our work for many years. We are three professionals working in Portland, Oregon, who advocate for and provide support to boys in various settings. One of us is a licensed clinical social worker, one is a licensed professional counselor, and one is an associate professor of counseling and school psychology. All three of us are also parents of young boys.

This guidebook describes our approach to facilitating strengths-based groups for boys at local elementary schools and in private practice. In these groups, we introduce boys to new perspectives on what it means to be male, we help them to build the relational skills they need to become good men, and, importantly, we accomplish these goals in a way that supports and does not shame boys for who they are. Although the three of us are men, we fully support the idea that women are equally capable leaders of BAM! groups. We address specific suggestions for both women and men leaders later in the text.

As one of the focal points of this guidebook, we describe the ways in which we, as leaders, appropriately share with the boys in our groups the influences that have shaped our own development as boys and men. In this way, this book reflects our efforts to step consciously into our roles as mentors, counselors, and fathers. Here are three brief stories that we share with the boys in our BAM! groups. We have added a bit to each as a way to introduce ourselves to you, the reader.

As a boy I was a poor athlete. My own family teased me about how slow I was. My athletic claim to fame was when I hit a home run by tipping the ball and lodging it inside the opposing catcher's protective gear. The ball could not be found until I had rounded the bases. For the past 18 years, I have been counseling boys and their families on the full range of issues that draw boys into counseling. I have thoroughly researched the developmental and educational needs of boys and travel to schools in the Northwest sharing my knowledge.

**Howard Hiton, MS, LPC**

I grew up in Brooklyn. As a young biracial boy I faced many challenges of fitting in. I recall a time when my maleness was challenged for wearing a pink shirt. I was pushed to physically defend myself. For the past 7 years I have been the social worker in an urban school in Portland, Oregon, with a focus on character education. I have been facilitating boys groups for 6 years and am presently also building a private practice that focuses on working with boys.

**Stephen Grant, LCSW**

When I was 15 years old, I invited a girl to my birthday party who was the school's social outcast. At the party, I was taunted by one of my friends who thought that she didn't belong. I was both embarrassed to be taunted but also glad I invited her. I am now a professor of counseling and school psychology at Lewis and Clark College. I maintain an active presence in the community, facilitating boys groups and supervising graduate students in schools in the Portland metro area.

**Peter Mortola, PhD**

# About Our Work With Boys

In this guidebook, we are specifically highlighting and addressing the issues that boys face in their development. We are, however, very aware of the continuing issues that girls face in their own development and we support all efforts on their behalf. We believe that everyone will benefit when both girls and boys are assisted in ways that work for them to grow into healthy and contributing members of society.

When we started offering supportive groups for boys in schools there was, in fact, already a model in place for such groups being offered for girls. These groups were called "girls empowerment groups" and, in these groups, girls were encouraged to gain self-esteem by learning to take initiative in their lives and to challenge the limitations of the female role in society as represented in advertising and the media. One of our female colleagues asked us to start an equivalent group for boys and we jumped at the opportunity, building on similar work we had been doing for years in other settings. However, we were also told that naming the group the "boys empowerment group" would raise some eyebrows: Why would boys need to be empowered in a male-dominated society?

This is where we have come to stand on this issue: We see boys needing to be empowered to re-own aspects of their own emotional lives. We see boys needing to be empowered to accept themselves as they are outside the stereotypical notions of what a man is supposed to be like. We see a need for boys to be empowered to find alternatives to the oftentimes violent and oppressive influences of their development so that they can embrace more flexible, healthy, and supported stances in their lives and in society.

Here are three brief vignettes to introduce you to a few of the strengths and struggles of some of the boys with whom we have worked (throughout this book, all identifying information of the boys we describe has been changed or deleted):

Theo is an athletic, charismatic boy who is large for his age and who others in his class see as a leader. He very rarely sees his dad, who lives in another state, and he has been repeatedly accused of bullying other boys on the playground.

Paul is one of the most articulate and confident 11-year-old boys we have ever worked with. He thrives in school drama productions and has danced with a local ballet company, but he also often antagonizes other boys verbally and is, in return, antagonized by them.

Sorin is a quiet and perceptive boy who is new to his school. He likes to wear brightly colored clothes, though he has been teased harshly for it. He tends to not talk a lot, and both his teacher and mother have been worried that he is becoming a loner and that he has given up trying to make friends.

As you can see, we open our groups to a wide variety of boys who are all in some way struggling with the constraints and challenges of what it means to be male in our culture. We see ourselves as advocates and mentors for these boys by helping them take on and address these issues. In order to help these boys, we have needed to dig deeply into our own experience as men and as counselors—as well as into our scholarship as developing professionals—to expand our understanding of who boys are by their nature, as well as who they become by our nurturing in society. Through these efforts, we have developed and will share with you in this guidebook an approach to working with boys in a way that helps them develop new relational skills by building on the strengths they bring to us. We appreciate your interest in also being an advocate for boys, and we look forward to sharing with you what we have found.

This book is dedicated to
Sally, Liz and Win
and our six sons
Sawyer, Eli, Miles, Cole, Noah and Riley

## About This Guidebook

We think of this curriculum as a kind of adventurer's guide into the mostly uncharted territory of facilitating supportive, strengths-based groups for boys in schools and community settings. We offer ideas for routes and pathways to interesting adventures and reasons why such adventures are important. Our hope is that this guidebook will serve as a kind of map for you to use as you navigate the challenging and rewarding work of mentoring and counseling boys. Our guidebook provides both the big ideas that orient our work—why we go down this path at all—and the small details of how we plan for and lead each week's adventures in order to accomplish our goals and arrive at our destinations. This guidebook is divided into three sections:

> BAM! Orientation
> BAM! Example
> BAM! Instructions

In BAM! Orientation, we present data that describe the challenges that boys are facing interpersonally and academically. We then outline some of the factors, biological as well as cultural, that influence boys' development. We also describe the ways we have found to work with boys in ways that address the challenges they face while still building on their strengths. We conclude this section with an outline of the goals we have for the work we do with boys in our groups.

In BAM! Example, we tell the story of our experience facilitating a particular BAM! group of 11 boys as it developed over a 10-week period. These week-by-week narratives illustrate the rich texture of our experience working with boys while bringing to life the theories and goals behind our work. In these stories, you will get to know some of the boys we have worked with, their struggles, and the relationships we developed with them over time as we both succeeded and stumbled in our efforts to connect with them.

In BAM! Instructions, we provide the detailed curriculum you will need to recreate the activities for each of the 10 group sessions described in the previous section. We also share with you the objectives, planning considerations, and prompts for processing each activity. In addition, we also highlight the role of the group facilitator—including advice for both men and women leaders—and discuss the nuts and bolts of beginning a BAM! group. Lastly, we provide evaluation forms and further ideas for you to use in your work with boys.

Our primary goal for this guidebook is to provide you with a strengths-based and positive approach to understanding boys and working with them in groups. It may seem contradictory, then, that our next section focuses on the challenges and problems that boys face in their development. We know that boys are already too often seen as problems and requiring participation in groups addressing such issues as anger management, social skills, and pregnancy prevention. While we believe that boys, on average, do need to learn more effective ways of meeting the world, we also believe that the world needs to learn to meet boys more helpfully as well. This is our challenge in this guidebook: to present a model of understanding and working with boys that is realistic about addressing the problems they face while also providing a positive and strengths-based approach to working with them.

We believe you will find this guidebook both thought provoking and practical, and we hope it inspires you to imagine new possibilities for the boys with whom you work.

# BAM! Orientation

## The Challenges Boys Face

Who hasn't marveled at the natural exuberance of boys? We watch with amazement as they skateboard for countless hours, run with boundless energy, and express unbridled enthusiasm for their latest interest. Young boys are often eager to please their teachers, free with expressions of love, and open with their expressions of tears and sadness. Picture a little boy stricken with grief over Old Yeller's death in the classic movie. Imagine how a little boy trembles with excitement as he lines up his cars in just the right way or builds a cool Lego contraption. Recall an image of a group of boys as they, in their excitable goofiness, fall over one another like puppies and amuse one another with wacky boy humor.

Most boys, when they are very young, are fully engaged in the world. They are in full contact with their own inner lives and experiences, their feelings, thoughts, and imaginings. They are also in full contact with the environment around them, literally poking it, touching it, and climbing all over it.

But then something happens as these young boys grow older. They start to lose their enthusiastic contact with important aspects of both their inner and outer life: They lose touch with certain emotions, they struggle to participate authentically in relationships with significant others, and many of them begin to lose touch with the meaning and purpose of schooling.

To put it bluntly, boys, on average, are struggling in significant ways both academically and relationally. In higher education, women now outnumber men as both enrollees and graduates. According to the National Center for Education Statistics (2005), girls are also outperforming boys in terms of grades not only in college, but also at the elementary, secondary, and high school levels.

Given these statistics, it is perhaps not surprising that only 44% of high school boys compared with 54% of girls report that they do at least 1 hour of homework per night, and only 55% of boys versus 68% of girls report that they are motivated to do well in school (Benson, Roehlkepart, & Leffert, 1997). Boys

1

are also 30% more likely than girls to flunk or drop out of school (National Center for Education Statistics, 2005). As a measure of the ultimate and tragic form of "dropping out," boys also account for 86% of all suicides between the ages of 15 and 24 (Anderson & Smith, 2003).

One place where you will find more boys than girls in schools is in special education classrooms (Soifer, 2002). Special education programs in public schools across the United States have been described as "largely a boys club" with twice as many boys being identified as requiring such services than girls (Vaishnav & Dedman, 2002). It is important to note that this "boy imbalance" in special education populations grows even greater as the diagnosis becomes more subjective. For example, boys are only slightly more likely to receive the objectively measured label of "hearing impaired," but they are more than twice as likely to be labeled "learning disabled" and more than three times as likely to receive the highly subjective label of being "emotionally disturbed."

This tendency for boys to be viewed as having more emotional and social problems than girls is also seen in the data collected on behavior rating scales used in schools throughout the country. Using these scales in both elementary and high schools, teachers and parents predominantly identify boys as possessing glaring deficits in social skills such as "cooperation," "empathy," and "study skills." Sadly, boys are also seen as possessing significantly greater problems in the areas of "aggression," "attention problems" and "hyperactivity" (Merrell & Popinga,1994; Reynolds & Kamphaus, 1992).

The link between boys and the diagnosis of attention deficit with hyperactivity disorder (ADHD) is one of the clearest examples of how young males are seen as problems in our schools and communities. In the United States, boys are up to three times more likely to be both referred and diagnosed for ADHD (Barkley, 1998). In some school systems within the United States, up to 20% of boys in the school's population are receiving psycho-stimulant medications for ADHD (Castellanos, Lee, & Sharp, 2002). Perhaps the most sobering statistics are these: With less than 5% of the world's population, the U.S. now accounts for 85% of the world's consumption of Ritalin, and 90% of all children taking Ritalin in the United States are boys (Pollack, 1998). The rise of the use of Ritalin within the United States has been exponential over the past two decades. "No country besides America is experiencing such a rise in Ritalin use," states Lawrence Diller, MD, in *Running on Ritalin* (1999). "It brings into question our cultural standards for behavior, performance and punishment; it highlights the most basic psychological aspects of nature versus nurture" (p. 23).

Clearly, boys are facing some real problems and they are in need of real help. Facing such a myriad of problems both academically and socially, it is perhaps no joke that males have also been found to smile less than females in social situations across the lifespan (LaFrance & Hecht, 2000). With so many problems being attributed to boys, attempting to help them can be overwhelming. Where do we begin to help boys with their struggles? How can we in the counseling and teaching professions approach boys as anything other than problems? In this next section, we share our insights on these two fundamental questions.

# The Necessity of Good Contact

...it is at the edge of anything, system or medium, that the most interesting events take place.

**David Holmgren, Permaculture cofounder (2007)**

We have just outlined how boys, on average, are facing significant challenges in three broad areas: (1) successfully engaging in schools (e.g., problems with academic success, learning disabilities, dropout rates); (2) successfully engaging in interpersonal relationships (e.g., problems with cooperation, empathy, attention deficit disorder); and (3) successfully engaging in the regulation of their own emotional lives (e.g., problems with emotional disturbance, aggression, and suicide). A close reading of these three broad problem areas reveals "successful engagement" as the common underlying thread: Boys are losing touch. Boys are tending to lose contact with themselves, with others, and with schools. We therefore see this basic issue of helping boys make better contact with themselves, with others, and with school systems as our primary goal in our work with boys in BAM! groups. In the following paragraphs, we define and describe this foundational idea of "contact" that grounds our thinking and our approach to working with boys.

Underlying many of the problems boys face—alienation from school, difficulties managing social interactions, and problems with emotional regulation—is the more fundamental problem of their disconnection from their own emotional experience as well as the social environment that surrounds them. The Gestalt notion of contact (Mortola, 2006) offers a useful model to understand how boys become disconnected and provides a theoretical basis for remedying their disconnection.

From a Gestalt perspective, healthy contact takes place at the boundary where the individual meets the world (Perls, Hefferline, & Goodman, 1951; Wheeler, 1991). We make good contact with the world using all of the aspects of our organism: our senses, our emotions, and our minds. Good contact is necessary for us to engage with the environments that surround us—both natural and social—and to get our needs met.

For example, when Ramon, a boy in one of our groups, lost a valued pet and needed some support, he reached out to us emotionally. He made eye contact with us and he spoke eloquently about his loss and what his dog Rudy had meant to him. He conveyed his loss in a way that allowed us to empathize with him. He used an appropriate tone of voice, congruent facial expressions, and the poignant movement of his hands to show how he used to hold Rudy in his arms when he was a puppy.

By using his body, his emotions, and his thoughts in such a "contactful" way, Ramon strengthened our relationship to him. We felt close to him, we were able to empathize with him, and we were therefore able to respond to him in ways that were helpful. After Ramon had finished speaking, for example, another boy in the group described how he also had cried when his pet bird had died, thus "normalizing" Ramon's feelings of grief. The whole group also attended to Ramon during these minutes and gave him the time and attention he needed to feel supported. In these ways, Ramon was able to leave the group that day feeling a little less alone, a little less sad, and a little more connected.

As Ramon demonstrates, good contact is the ability to be fully engaged with our world. Good contact with the *self*, however, is also a necessary aspect of making good contact. Ramon couldn't have asked for understanding about his own experience of grief if he wasn't first aware of and in good contact with his own feelings of being sad and lonely. Ramon demonstrated good contact with himself through his ready awareness of his own thoughts, feelings, and needs. In this way, Ramon provides us with an excellent example of how good contact is both the ability to be in touch with one's own inner experiences and the ability to communicate one's experience in appropriate ways in the world in order to get one's needs met.

Simply put, we know good contact when we see it: Contact looks like presence and may reflect a multitude of feelings, it is animated, and it is an honest representation of a person's inner world. Contact is knowing who you are inside and bringing that knowledge to interact with others. It is showing up fully, being present, allowing others in, and letting yourself out. Contact is possible when we allow ourselves to be vulnerable, to be "in touch." In contrast, the inability to make good contact looks frozen, insensitive, guarded, stoic, and aloof. Not surprisingly, these are the very words we use to describe the stance of traditional masculinity.

So how do boys begin to lose contact with themselves and the world around them? In this next section we address the social influences on boys that limit their ability to maintain good contact as they grow and develop.

# The Social Influences: The Impact of Dysfunctional Aspects of Traditional Masculinity on Boys' Relationships

As we have noted, boys enter the world full of zest and fully "in contact" with the world and with themselves. Their desire to connect with other people gets expressed in the strong attachments they form with their family members, other caring adults, and their peers. As boys age, relationships with other boys become particularly important. Research findings from the psychological literature show that boys' friendships tend to be stable and characterized by mutual support and companionship shared through active and competitive types of activities (Buhrmester, 1996; Camarena, Sarigiani, & Petersen, 1990; McNelles & Connolly, 1999). These friendships are vital to a boy's well-being.

Unfortunately, some boys are exposed to a harsh socialization process that forces them to internalize outdated and dysfunctional notions of masculinity that can impair their ability to make deep emotional connections with others. Although males generally are more like than unlike females in their emotions (Wester et al., 2002), many boys are taught that emotional openness is a liability. Subject to challenges such as "boys don't cry" (i.e., men don't show vulnerability) and shaming taunts if they do cry (e.g., "Don't be a girly-man!"), many boys learn to censor aspects of themselves that they fear do not meet the social expectations for "being a man" (Pollack, 1998).

Although there are certainly variations across cultural, ethnic, and socioeconomic groups (Way & Chu, 2004), we believe there are pervasive, dysfunctional aspects of traditional masculinity that influence many boys throughout the United States. These limiting and dysfunctional aspects of traditional masculinity are media influenced—the muscles of G.I. Joe "play action figures," for example, are 30 times larger now than they were when first sold (Pope et al., 1999)—and they affect the lives of boys from many different backgrounds, unnecessarily constricting their definition of what a man is supposed to be and how a man is supposed to act.

We have detailed a complete and harrowing list of these limiting cultural messages that many boys receive through their socialization in week 6 of BAM! Example. Boys who internalize these dysfunctional beliefs regarding masculinity become convinced that expressing vulnerability is not cool, and crying about the loss of a pet, for example, is certainly not permitted. Guarding against shame, many boys develop a coat of armor to protect themselves against ridicule and humiliation. The armor boys wear may serve as a defense against what they see as a threatening world, but it also separates them from necessary contact—from their own experience and from the ability to connect authentically with others.

This process of armoring eventually teaches some boys to deny their own experience and results in a loss of contact with their own internal compass, leaving them susceptible to peer pressure and unwise influences. Unable to navigate their own emotional landscape, these boys are in danger of not only losing touch with how to care for themselves in healthy ways, but also with knowing how to appropriately empathize with others. If Ramon was feeling lonely and sad, for example, but couldn't identify, respect, and "own" those feelings, he may have pushed them away as something only "sissies" feel. Lacking access to and ownership of his own feelings, Ramon would not only lose touch with himself, he would also begin to lose the ability to connect empathetically with others in similar situations.

We have seen the results of these internalized social pressures to conform to an unrealistic, unhealthy, and limited standard of what it means to be a man ripple out in numerous ways in our practice.

A parent calls to set up an initial counseling appointment and says, "My son used to excel in school. He was in the talented and gifted program. Now he is in middle school and is getting Cs and Ds. I don't know how to talk to him. He just doesn't seem to care. He seems so unhappy."

A 14-year-old boy discusses the impact of getting teased when he was younger. He remembers the time when he began to build his tough façade to endure the teasing. He acknowledges how this façade has led him to harden, to be less friendly, and to be more of a loner. He demonstrates some understanding of the dilemma this creates when speaking about switching schools and hoping to make new friends. "I don't know what I am going to do. You can't be too open but you can't be a total dick either," he says.

A 20-year-old discloses that he uses marijuana daily because he feels anxious and scared. He says that he could never reveal his feelings of vulnerability to his friends out of fear of being humiliated. So he hides his feelings and continues to use marijuana instead of being honest about his experience.

We see many boys at about the age of 12 beginning to censor themselves, imagining they need to be tougher and cooler than they actually are. Following the lead and copying the mannerisms of older boys, these younger ones begin to strive for a cool indifference rather than a warm connectedness. This is why we have focused our efforts on fifth-grade boys: to give them a group social experience in which their quickly limiting definition of what it means to be a man can be expanded to include the relational and communicative abilities to make healthy contact with themselves and the world around them.

We have stated that many boys receive clear messages from the culture that limit their abilities to make good contact with themselves and with the world around them. These boys get put in a box that is too small for them, and they end up lopping off important aspects of themselves in order to conform and fit to that constricted definition of masculinity.

We think there is another aspect of the way that many boys are socialized that creates problems for them in their development: If boys were books, they are being misread and misinterpreted. Through this misreading and misunderstanding of who boys are by their nature, we are tending to treat and socialize boys in our nurturing in ways that are not helpful to them.

On the whole, for example, boys seem to process emotions differently than girls (Manstead, 1992). Researchers have found that boys tend to get overwhelmed by strong emotions and, when facing potent feelings, may appear to shut down. In one relevant study (Kraemer, 2000), 6-year-old boys and girls were placed in a room by themselves and played an audiotape of a baby in distress. On initial observation it appeared that the girls had a stronger emotional reaction than the boys. Researchers observed the girls being visibly upset and attempting to comfort the crying baby. Boys, on the other hand, displayed a flat affect or even turned off the switch that played the tape.

At first glance, this appears to support a stereotype that boys are unfeeling and callous. However, on closer examination, the researchers found that internal measures of agitation such as heart rate and sweat response revealed that boys were *more* agitated than girls. It appears that the boys in this study were besieged by a strong emotional reaction and attempted to end their discomfort by shutting down any outward signs of emotions and by turning off the tape.

In addition to boys' demonstrations of apparent apathy, we have found in our own work with boys that they may react with anger or defensiveness when overwhelmed with vulnerable emotions. This may come as no surprise given the effects of being "put in the box," as we described earlier. Wouldn't you react defensively if you were socialized to believe, as many boys are, that you should never feel vulnerable and certainly not appear that way?

Most boys, then, are actually having and processing the normal range of human emotions, but it may not look that way from the outside. Because of this incongruity between what boys are feeling and what they are showing, we may tend to take boys' demonstrations of apathy or anger at face value and fail to look deeper. Assuming that boys aren't vulnerable, and that they don't need us, we may allow ourselves to be pushed away by what appears to be boys' indifference. What we fail to see is that boys' demonstrations of anger and apathy are often a defense against emotions that overwhelm them.

When we view boys' indifference as evidence they are tough, strong, unemotional, and don't need contact with others, we fail them and contribute to their disconnection, their lack of contact. We believe it is essential to recognize that boys, too, have an inner emotional life, even though it may be difficult to get to. Some boys may need particular help in understanding and navigating that emotional world, and many may need guidance and practice to develop their emotional muscles that are weak from disuse or disregard.

We have stated that there are two strong negative influences in the socialization of many boys: (1) they are "put in a box" that limits the range of their emotional and behavioral repertoires, and (2) their particular way of processing or responding to emotions is "misread," and we therefore distance ourselves and lose contact with them. Both of these influences challenge a boy's ability to directly address and discuss anything that might make him appear vulnerable in the company of others. How, then, do you set up a group experience for boys wherein it is okay to both feel and express vulnerability and, therefore, to make authentic contact with one another?

We have had to be thoughtful about this over time. We learned from early failures that boys in general were not comfortable with the traditional group counseling methods that we learned in graduate school, such as sitting quietly in a circle and discussing feelings face-to-face with others. We learned that traditional counseling processes and approaches were often, in fact, a "damned if you do, damned if you don't" experience for boys: they have learned to feel shame for showing vulnerability, now they are shamed if they aren't able to show it to us in counseling (Tannen, 1994).

What we discovered was that in order to help boys redress their relational constraints imposed on them by our nurturing, we needed to support the way they make contact naturally. We learned from experience and research that boys, in general, had a biologically influenced style of making contact that we had to understand and respect. In short, we learned that, to help boys make better contact, we needed to make better contact with them. In the next section we detail the biological influences of what we have come to call a boy's "contact style."

# The Biological Influences: A Different Kind of Contact for Boys

Earlier, we described what good interpersonal contact looks like: It involves an awareness of one's own emotional state and the ability to clearly communicate those emotions and needs. This clear communication involves verbal statements, congruent nonverbal communication—such as direct eye contact—and an appropriately expressive physical presence that helps one be understood. We believe these types of contact skills are crucial if one is to meet the world appropriately in order to get one's needs met. These relational skills, in fact, have become even more important as the world has become more populated and with more of us living in crowded urban centers. In addition, over time, traditional gender roles have become more flexible: More women are in the business world, and more men are caring for the young and involving themselves in the difficult work of parenting. For these reasons, we believe our work with young boys to help them develop their relational and communication skills is key.

The first few years we facilitated BAM! groups, we expected boys to practice and demonstrate these types of contactful behaviors right off the bat. It didn't take us long to learn that this was the wrong approach. One year early on, we started off the first session of our group by having the boys sit in a circle, face to face, and "check in" by telling us a bit about themselves. What we got instead of friendly sharing and warm contact in the group was a series of clipped, sarcastic, and critical comments accompanied by the nonverbal communication of cool and closed physical gestures and postures. The temperature in the room and in the group dropped quickly and never really recovered.

We now see the failure of that early opening exercise not only as a deficit in the range of social skills boys are able to demonstrate, but also as a deficit in our own understanding of what has been described as a boy's relational style (Kiselica, 2001, 2003) or what we will further define as a boy's "contact style." That is, we realized that both the boys and us as leaders had a new language to learn. Boys might need to improve their skills supporting good interpersonal contact, but we needed to learn about a boy's preferred style of communication, relationship, and contact.

We now know that boys come into the world attending to—and making contact with—particular things in particular ways. We have learned that if we want to succeed in helping boys become more relational and contactful with themselves and the world around them, we need to have a better understanding of, respect for, and ability to work with these tendencies.

Like many professionals trained in the social sciences over the past 30 years, we used to think that boys and girls would reflect the same interests and develop the same social skills if we socialized them all equally. That is, we believed that boys would respond just as well to dolls and be less interested in wheels if we were just careful enough about which toys we chose for them to play with. As we will show, research over the past few decades has done much to debunk this myth that all behavioral, sex-related differences have roots in socialization.

As BAM! group leaders, we still maintain a hearty respect for the influences of socialization (as evidenced in the previous section on the social influences of boys' development), but we have also come to see that ignoring a boy's natural "contact style" is dangerous: If we don't know how to make contact with boys, how do we expect them to make contact with us? Here is a story from Peter's experience as a new father that highlights this point:

> When my son Noah was just a few months old, I began to notice that he didn't make much eye contact with me. From all the reading I had done, I was expecting him to gaze deeply into my eyes as I gazed into his. But instead Noah seemed to prefer staring at shadows on the wall and was seemingly unaware of and indifferent to my presence. With my training in psychology, I was too quick to wonder if these were early signs of autism. I also couldn't help but notice that I felt like making less contact with him because he didn't seem to be that interested in making contact with me. Now that Noah is a smiling, talking, fully relational 2-year-old, I can laugh at the fears and concerns I had back then. But I also have learned that there was something about Noah— and about boys in general—that I needed to better understand.

What all three have us have come to learn about boys is that they may not always make contact with us in the way we expect or want them to. After Peter's experience with Noah, for example, we learned that, from the first day of birth onward, infant baby boys have shown a preference for looking at a mobile hanging over their crib rather than a human face that is gazing at them (Lutchmaya & Baron-Cohen, 2002).

Throughout childhood, adolescence, and adulthood, in fact, females have demonstrated much greater interest in and success with "reading faces" (Hall, 1984; Hall, Carter, & Horgan, 2000; McClure, 2000; Woods, 1996). Women, for example, will take more time to consider what someone else's facial expression is communicating, and they will respond with more emotional arousal to that facial expression than a man will (Orozco & Ehlers, 1998). Additionally, watching a cartoon of two characters interacting, toddler girls will use more words to describe the mental and affective states of those characters, and they will also make more efforts to describe the intentions of those characters (Knickmeyer & Wheelwright, 2005). In these ways, girls tend to be better at the kind of "mind reading" that is essential for making good contact and empathizing with others (Baron-Cohen, 2003; Baron-Cohen et al., 2003).

To underscore the contributions of biology in this discussion, consider the following: All human babies start out as female in the womb. In the first few weeks of development, some babies become boys by being "marinated" in testosterone and androgens. Researchers are now able to show that those baby boys who were influenced by higher levels of prenatal testosterone show lower levels of eye contact and produce less vocabulary by the time they are walking and talking toddlers (Lutchmaya, Baron-Cohen, & Raggat, 2002a, 2002b).

This tendency for girls to have a larger vocabulary and be stronger in various aspects of language use has also been demonstrated across the lifespan, and, importantly, estrogen is implicated in this strength (Institute of Medicine, 2001). Estrogen is the hormone that most influences girls in the same way that testosterone is the hormone that most influences boys. When estrogen is at its peak influence at ovulation in the monthly female cycle, for example, females tend to be better at tasks related to retrieval of language from memory (Kuhlmann & Wolf, 2005). Interestingly, Koko, the female lowland gorilla famous for her use of sign language, also made more efforts at communication and produced more signs when she was at the peak of her cycle as well (Patterson, Holts, & Saphire, 1991). A similar finding related to the connection of language skills and language relates to menopause in women: When estrogen's presence and influence decline in menopause, so does the edge that women have over men in terms of verbal fluency, naming, and articulation. However, when a woman receives estrogen replacement therapy, her verbal advantages over men return (Kimura, 1995).

If boys tend to not read faces and emotions as well as girls do, or use verbal communication as effusively or effectively, to what are they attending and how do they communicate? What does a boy's preferred contact style look like, and how can it be seen from a strengths-based perspective rather than from a deficit model?

Like Noah gazing at the mobile in the earlier story, boys seem to attend slightly more to "effect" rather than "affect." Put another way, they seem to attend more toward the "motion" in the world and a little bit less toward the "emotion" in the world. From very early on in infancy, boys have shown a tendency to gravitate toward toys that move rather than toys that have faces (Knickmeyer & Wheelwright, 2005). By the time they are toddlers, boys also have shown a strong tendency to prefer films about moving cars rather than films portraying faces that talk (Connellan, 2001).

Captive male Vervet monkeys have also been shown to have this same tendency to play with cars instead of dolls (Alexandera, 2002), lending support to the theory that early in our evolution as mammals, it became advantageous for males and females to attend to—to make contact with—differing aspects of the environment. That is, most female primates show strengths in attending to the relational and communicative aspects of mothering—paying close attention to the expressive faces and demonstrated needs of newborns in particular, while most male primates show strengths in attending to the visual and spatial aspects of the surrounding environment—i.e., things that move and that could either be a source of food or a potential threat (Wright, 1994).

As in our previous example regarding boys' tendencies to gaze at mobiles rather than faces, it is important to note the role of biology in this differentiation of toy selection and attentional differences in boys and girls. For example, girls born with congenital adrenal hyperplasia (CAH) have experienced very high levels of testosterone in the womb. Although this hormone imbalance is usually corrected at birth, later in childhood girls born with CAH show strong preferences for what experimenters identify as "boy-typical" toys such as those involved in transportation and construction tasks (Berenbaum, 2000). Girls born with CAH also score unusually high on tests of spatial awareness and orientation which usually tend to be strengths for males on such tests (Berenbaum & Resnick, 1997).

Boys not only tend to pay more attention to things that move, they themselves also tend to move more than girls do. As most parents of boys can attest, infant boys are more active than girls, especially when it comes to the activation of large muscle groups such as those involved in throwing and running (Junaid & Fellowes, 2006). These differences between boys' and girls' activity levels also have been shown to increase during childhood (Eaton & Enns, 1986).

In addition, boys have demonstrated a strong preference for a more "rough and tumble" style of play than girls do (Maccoby, 1998). "Rough and tumble play," of course, is a euphemism for "aggressive play." In countries around the world, boys have been shown, in fact, to demonstrate higher levels of aggression (such as pushing, hitting, and grabbing) than girls do (Munroe et al., 2000). And while it is true that the number of aggressive acts performed by boys tends to be greater in countries where boys are socialized in more traditional gender roles (thereby highlighting the influence of socialization on aggression), it is also true that this tendency for boys to be more aggressive has shown up in each country where it has been measured (thereby highlighting the role of biology in this tendency).

Let's summarize what we have stated so far regarding the biological influences on a boy's particular contact style: Boys seem to have a tendency to make contact with the world in a way that differs not only from girls, but also from adult expectations of what good contact should look like. That is, boys on the whole tend to use less direct eye contact, they tend to not read emotions on faces as well, they tend to use less verbal communication, and they tend to be more physically active and even aggressive in the way that they engage in the world. In short, boys in general tend to not produce the kinds of contactful behaviors that we expect of children as they sit in classrooms or in the counselor's office.

On average, then, a boy's "contact style" with the world may not look like contact at all. That is, in a social situation where you hope to have his complete attention, a boy may tend to squirm and fidget, not looking you in the eye, and produce far fewer empathetic statements than you might hope. Spelled out in this way, it is easy to understand how boys are seen as having fewer relational and social skills and less ability to make good contact with themselves and others. Their contact skills are not only limited by their socialization as males, but their contact skills seem to also be particularized by their biology.

We think it is very important at this point, however, to assert our "boy positive" stance: We do not see boys as broken girls when it comes to relational and communication skills (Heesacker et al., 1999). We do see that they have relational challenges—stemming from both biological and social influences—with which they need our help and encouragement. But we have also come to appreciate that a boy's contact style has its own strengths as well, as we describe in the next section. If we want to help boys make better contact, we have to learn to make better contact with them.

# Seeing Boys' Strengths and Addressing Their Challenges

I note the obvious differences between each sort and type, but we are more alike, my friends, than we are unalike.

**Maya Angelou,** *Human Family* **(1990)**

We have just highlighted the social and biological influences on what we have called a boy's "contact style." We have described the ways in which socialization limits a boy's relational capacities to make good contact and we have also described the ways that biology influences the particular kind of contact that a boy tends to make. We have summarized—and oversimplified—this difference by stating that boys tend more toward *effect* rather than *affect*. Having highlighted these differences, however, we now return to similarities.

As in Maya Angelou's quote, we think that boys and girls are actually more similar than they are different. All human beings around the globe share common characteristics that make us fundamentally human. We are all born needing the support of and attachment to significant adults, and, furthermore, we are born with the innate relational capacities to develop these attachments (Siegel, 1999).

Around the world, men and women share the same facial expressions that communicate essentially the same basic emotions of joy, sadness, fear, disgust, anger, and surprise—and multiple complex variations on those emotive themes (Brown, 1991). Affect theory (Tomkins, 1962), in fact, tells us that, for all of us, such emotions and their expressions are the manner with which we either reach out (e.g., feeling joy) or withdraw from the environment (e.g., disgust) in our ongoing process of regulating our needs.

We want to stress that boys as well as girls share all these basic capacities for relationship, emotion, and regulation (Kiselica & O'Brien, 2001). Furthermore, despite all the controversy over how different our brains may be, women and men share all the same basic cognitive functions as well as, on average, the same general levels of intelligence (Halpern, 2005). We state these similarities because we do not think that boys and girls should be treated or viewed as a different kind of animal all together. We see boys and girls, in fact, sharing nearly completely overlapping sets of skills and attributes with only slight differences at the edges of their skill sets.

Simon Baron-Cohen (2003) has used the image of two overlapping bell curves to help us think about how boys and girls are mostly the same, but in some small but significant ways different. He describes how boys tend to be more skilled as "systemitizers" (i.e., slightly more interested in the aspects of cause and effect within all kinds of systems, from cars to computers) and that girls tend to be more skilled as "empathizers" (i.e., slightly more able to read the complex emotional currents and interpersonal processes within human relationships). The key point here, however, is that boys are not one thing and girls another: Sex differences are not an "either/or" proposition. That is, most human beings are good at both systemizing and empathizing, and most human beings are interested in effect as well as affect. It's just that, by nature, boys tend to lean in one direction of interest and girls tend to lean in another. Baron-Cohen emphasizes, as we do, that these differences are apparent "on average" in human populations and that variation and strengths may be different for any given individual, whether boy or girl.

In this way, we need to appreciate how boys and girls are mostly the same. We would be missing something important, however, if we did not recognize that boys and girls may have tendencies in contact styles that reflect both strengths and weaknesses. It is clear, for example, that a girl's tendency to be better at empathy and relational skills is a benefit to her in the complexly social and interpersonal aspects of our present-day world. It is also clear from research over the past 10 years (Burr, Ostrov, & Jansen, 2005; Crick, 1996), however, that a girl's edge in verbal skills and subtle relational understandings over boys in general can also present her with particular challenges. Nicki Crick and her colleagues (Crick & Grotpeter, 1995) have been documenting, for example, the ways in which girls can and do use their verbal and relational acuity to, at times, act in clearly harmful and aggressive ways in their relationships with other girls. In these studies, girls report that they use such "relational aggression" because of how important it is for them to feel included, to have a sense of belonging and connectedness with their peers. In this way, a relational challenge for a girl may be to learn to stand more independently and, ironically, to care *less* about belonging to a group. We also know that girls suffer significantly higher rates of anxiety, panic disorders, and depression than boys do during adolescence (Hankin & Abramson, 1999). In this way, it may also be important for a girl to learn to be more assertive and externalizing (as opposed to the internalizing tendencies that these maladies represent) in expressing her independent wants and needs as well as being assertive about getting them met.

We know from the data presented earlier that a boy's relational and contact style brings different challenges. For example, many boys need to learn to be more cooperative and less aggressive, as well as less violent, in expressing their wants and needs. Additionally, they need practice in attending to and verbalizing their own needs, as well as attending to the expressed emotions and needs of others.

We have found, however, that there is less affirmation as to the strengths that a boy's particular contact style may provide. In our work with boys in BAM! groups, we have seen these strengths at work in many different ways and in many different situations. Their tendency toward effect, for example, is demonstrated as a positive social skill in their quick readiness to work at solving problems as both individuals and groups (see our description of the Electric Fence in week 1 of BAM! Example). Their high levels of activity (aka "squirreliness") in our groups also bring high levels of positive energy, eager participation, humor, and risk taking to our experiences together.

Even though the boys we work with may not be as comfortable with face-to-face communication as noted by Tannen (1990), we have found that when we create activities for them to do with each other, side by side and shoulder to shoulder, their phobias about appearing vulnerable disappear and they are able to literally hold and support one another in surprising ways (see our example of Trust Falling in week 8 of BAM! Example).

We have also learned to reframe a boy's tendency to adore cars and trucks as reflecting a kind of social skill as well. We have pointed out in our work with boys, for example, the essential service to the community that the driver of a garbage truck provides. We have also talked about the intricate orchestration of communication with others that an operator of a large crane engages in on a daily basis. On a related side note, one boy we spoke to recently also described how much more important he felt after we helped him see his deep interest in software programming as actually reflecting the larger social skill of wanting to help people work together better on important projects.

As BAM! leaders, we have also come to realize that, by honoring and channeling a boy's naturally high level of aggression, we can see a surprising social skill in what is normally viewed as pathology. Boys in our groups literally come into the room tumbling over one another, for example, and we have had to learn to reframe this as sometimes being a good thing. At the end of the first week of one new group, a 10-year-old boy named Jonah expressed that one thing he liked about the group so far was that he had made a new friend in Dana, another 10-year-old boy. As soon as the two of them came into the room for the second session the following week, Jonah ended up on top of Dana after a brief wrestling tussle, Dana's smiling face literally being smashed into the foam mat we had thoughtfully provided. Although Jonah's behavior clearly could be seen as aggressive, it was Dana's smiling face that told us that Jonah's way of making affectionate if rambunctious contact was being accepted, even appreciated. Sometimes, making and keeping friends looks different for a boy. We have learned that, unless someone is getting hurt, we need to honor that difference.

On a more serious note, we have also had moments in our groups where we find ourselves walking a fine line in supporting a boy's aggression—like when one boy described stepping in to break up a fight where his younger sibling was being pummeled by an older boy, for example—while at the same time taking a stand against the use of violence as a solution to problems. We have found, though, that boys are hungry to talk about such important distinctions and that our conversations and shared stories help them address these concerns (see the pink shirt story in week 5 of BAM! Example).

To summarize what we have stated in this section regarding our appreciation of the strengths of a boy's contact style: We believe that a boy's contact style may not look like we expect. Boys seem to make better contact standing side by side, for example, than face to face. Boys may even be able to show paradoxically more affection on the wrestling mat than through the spoken word. A boy's relational skills may be more easily expressed indirectly through things than directly toward others. The boys we have worked with have demonstrated their rich contact and social skills in their tendencies to be quick to move toward solving problems, to be full of high energy, to be willing to take risks, to be willing to be assertive—even aggressive—in pro-social ways, and to be deeply engaged in interests that serve, perhaps indirectly, the larger social good. So how do we build on these skills in our work with boys to help them gain some level of competency in some of the relational skills they may lack? We give some pointers in the following section.

# Five Goals for BAM! Leaders: Making Better Contact With Boys

As we have described, we believe that there are many positive aspects of a boy's relational style—and about boys in general—that are often overlooked in our clamor regarding what they lack. In highlighting these strengths, we are not ignoring the clear needs and challenges that boys face regarding making better contact with themselves and others. By focusing on these strengths, however, we have found that we can harness and direct their natural tendencies and strengths in the service of shoring up their relational skill deficits. In this way, we get the best of both worlds: The boys learn new relational skills, and they, in turn, want to come to our groups because they are fun and engaging.

Based on the relational strengths we have been describing, we want to share with you five specific, strengths-based approaches to working with boys that we have found help us make better contact with them. We have come to think of these approaches as our own goals as group leaders in working with boys. These five goals also serve to summarize what we have learned from the research we have described on both the social and biological influences on a boy's contact style, as well as how we have applied this knowledge in our practice with boys.

1. **Contradict limiting social messages:** Help boys out of the box. Boys grow up hearing messages about what it means to be a man. These messages are often limiting and hurtful (e.g., "boy's don't cry" and "boys need to prove themselves through fighting"). We need to help boys learn that there are many ways to be a man, that it is okay to own and express vulnerable feelings, and that there are many ways to resolve conflicts other than through hurtful violence. Help the boys you know to feel valued and respected for who they are, whether they play football or dance ballet, whether they hunt or knit.

2. **Respect indirectness:** Shoot baskets with boys first, talk later. Because of both biological and social reasons, boys tend to not be as direct in expressions of certain emotions. Help boys attend to and express their more vulnerable emotions by approaching them indirectly: Let them fiddle with something in their hands while you talk; shoot baskets while having a conversation; tell them about your own experiences before expecting them to tell you about theirs.

3. **Encourage directness:** Support and develop boys' relational skills.
   If boys tend to pay more attention to things like cars, wheels, and computers rather than faces, emotions, and relationships, they may need support and encouragement to develop and use their relational and communication skills: Teach the boys you know to look directly in someone's face to give or receive a compliment; help them understand what someone else is feeling and

how their facial expressions show it; discuss how a character in a movie might have felt; help them see how important it is for them to understand their own feelings in order to discover, ask for, and get what they need.

4. **Encourage regulation:** Teach boys to romp respectfully.

   Boys, on average, are more physically active and aggressive than girls. They need to be given opportunities to be physically expressive (e.g., active recesses at school, permission to engage in "rough and tumble" play, etc.) but they also need to learn to "hold back" on certain impulses (e.g., physically fighting, running around a classroom). This means we need to be actively engaged in teaching them how to regulate their own behaviors. It is not helpful to be completely "hands off" (i.e., "Oh, boys will be boys") or completely overcontrolling (e.g., expecting boys to sit quietly for extended periods of time).

5. **Notice the good:** See boys as something other than problems.

   We tend to highlight the trouble boys get into and forget to support them for the good things they bring to us. Realize that part of the problem boys have in meeting the world has to do with the way that the world meets them. Take an active interest in what boys find interesting and find a way to value it. Help them to see that the trucks and tractors they love actually help build houses. Help them to see that football is also about being part of a team, caring for your teammates, and doing something challenging and important together.

# Five Goals for BAM! Participants: Helping Boys Make Better Contact

In our introduction to this guidebook, we described how our challenge with this guidebook was to provide a positive and strengths-based approach to working with boys while also being realistic about addressing the problems they face. We have just outlined five specific ways of approaching boys that have helped us make better contact with them in positive ways that draw on their strengths and natural tendencies.

We next turn our attention to the five specific goals that we have targeted for the boys in our groups that help them address and shore up some of the relational challenges they face. As we have described, the ultimate goal of BAM! groups is to help boys experience healthy contact with themselves and others. We foster and develop this healthy contact through focusing on the following five specific objectives for the boys who are participants in our groups:

1. **Participants will increase their awareness of the social pressures boys face and broaden their notions of what it means to be a man.**

   Through discussion, activity, and facilitated dialogue, we expose the messages boys receive about what it means to be a man. Rather than simply conforming to unhealthy and limiting messages, we want boys to gain some ability to analyze and make choices about such messages. Boys are acutely aware of the social expectations placed on them as young men but have not had the guidance to put words to their experience. We want the boys in this group to be able to identify both positive and limiting social pressures on boys and men. Further, we want them to consider the broad range of personal qualities available to men.

2. **Participants will increase their sense of belonging, participation, and safety in a group.**

   There are few places for boys to let down their guard and relate to others authentically. Creating safe places for boys to be real is essential. In BAM! groups, boys are given this opportunity. Through activities that allow participants to identify, accept, and support similarities as well as differences among group members, boys experience themselves as unique but not alone. As a result, boys in our groups create and strengthen friendships within the group.

3. **Participants will improve their relational and communication skills.**

   Many of the problems boys face stem from the difficulties they have skillfully relating to others. BAM! group leaders choreograph experiences in which participants can be honest, respectful, and direct in their communication with both the adults and the boys in the group. We recognize when boys actively listen to and empathize with others in the group. Activities encourage the boys to work cooperatively with others in the group.

4. **Participants will expand emotional and behavioral repertoire.**

   We want boys to become more emotionally fluent. In BAM! groups, boys are coached to identify and express a broad range of emotions. At the same time, many boys have difficulties due to impulsive behavior and unchecked anger. Through initiatives, guided conversation, and direct instruction, boys are taught to more skillfully manage and regulate emotions like anger and behaviors like impulsivity and aggression.

5. **Participants will be able to carry the lessons from BAM! groups into other parts of their lives.**

   We want the lessons and experiences boys gain from these groups to make a difference in their lives now and in the future. The social pressures placed on boys are enormous. We work with them to increase their ability to use refusal skills, make healthy decisions, and choose good friends so that they have support to be healthy young men. We enlist the help of significant men in their lives to create a supportive bridge between the group and the boys' lives outside of the group. Lastly, we assist boys to identify personal strengths that they can draw on outside the group.

# A New Experience for Boys: Walking the Talk in BAM! Groups

According to the National Longitudinal Study on Adolescent Health, a survey of 12,000 young people across the country (Resnick 1997), a child's connection to a caring adult and that child's perception of his or her school as a caring environment are the strongest protection against high-risk behavior. BAM! groups represent our method of creating a caring school environment where connections with supportive adults and other boys are key.

BAM! groups are about both prevention and intervention. Contrary to the typical approach to boys, however, these groups are not focused on reducing a particular behavior. Instead, the goal of BAM! groups is to help boys become more emotionally literate and relationally competent while working with boys in ways that work for them. Too often boys in our society learn to interact with each other in ways that are hurtful, involve put-downs, and generally do not foster safe and supportive friendships. In contrast, BAM! groups create an environment where boys can feel safer with and more supported by one another, with less of a need to act aggressively or defensively. We want boys in these groups to use their naturally buoyant and expressive energies in mutually supportive ways in order to experience a positive sense of belonging, safety, and involvement on their playgrounds, in their classrooms, and in their communities.

In BAM! groups, we intentionally orchestrate a social environment wherein boys are encouraged to be honest with themselves, express a broad range of emotions, and relate more directly with their peers. If the typical school hallways socialize boys to be on guard, BAM! groups provide boys a social experience in which they can remove their armor.

We believe in the ability of boys to be healthy and happy individuals as well as positive contributors to community and family life. To achieve this, we must recognize and support what is natural about boys' behavior while helping them to be more relationally skilled and emotionally intelligent. This is not about making boys into girls. Whether boys are from urban, rural, or suburban settings, what is important is that they are emotionally healthy. Whether they play football or dance ballet, whether they hunt or knit, what matters is that boys are relationally competent.

As we have been describing, in order for us to help boys make better contact with themselves and others, we must first be able to connect with boys ourselves. Knowing about boys' preferences for communication and contact help us to make better connections with them. Because by nature and nurture boys may not approach emotional content as directly as girls, for example, we tend to work with them indirectly. We tell them our own stories before asking them to tell us theirs. We also work side by side with them in activities as much as we ask them to work with us or each other in a face-to-face manner. In general, we keep our communications with them playful, subtle, and casual.

By working with them in these indirect ways, we have often been surprised by the powerfully direct ways that boys will respond in the group. We ask them to physically support one another over an imaginary "electric fence" and they tell us afterward how they have learned to feel trust in one another. We tell them a story about losing one of our fathers, and one of the boys tells us how painful it has been to have not seen his mom since he was 3 years old.

Because we know that boys are concerned about being seen as vulnerable, we allow them outlets to dissipate the anxiety of being authentic in our groups. We have learned, for example, that allowing them to fidget with something in their hands and even gaze at the object while they are talking or listening paradoxically enhances their ability to make contact with us and each other.

We have discovered two major types of activities in our boys group that have been especially helpful in connecting with boys and in helping them connect with themselves and others: strategic storytelling and physical challenges. In the next sections, we describe our approach to using these two types of activities.

# Making Contact Through Strategic Storytelling

Strategic storytelling is a technique we use to make contact with boys using a conversational method that fits their communication preferences. We are aware that many schools of thought within counselor education programs emphasize the pitfalls of self-disclosure and typically recommend severely restricting its use. We know we are venturing into controversial territory here by advocating the use of facilitator self-disclosure in BAM! groups. In this section, we will explain our rationale for thoughtfully sharing personal stories in BAM! groups. We will also describe guidelines to ensure that the storytelling is effective and in the group's best interest.

What makes our approach to telling personal stories strategic is that we use narrative with specific intentions in mind. In the following paragraphs we expand on how storytelling in our groups helps us accomplish three things: Stories help us draw boys into better contact, they help us model contactful behavior on the part of the group leader, and they help us make abstract and complicated ideas more personal and engaging.

Storytelling and story listening draw people into connection. Sharing stories allows us as adult leaders to make good contact with the boys in our groups because the stories we tell allow the boys to see us as interesting, willing to be vulnerable, and as having been young once, too. As we tell stories we make contact with ourselves first by recalling the event we are talking about. Then we make contact with the boys by sharing our experience. Imagine the storyteller animated and present while an eager listener leans forward, silent and focused on the speaker's words. This is the very contact boys often lack being able to demonstrate and the type of contact we want them to have in these groups, not only with us but also with one another.

As we have noted, boys are often reluctant to discuss personal matters without first having authentic self-disclosure modeled. We have found that hearing a facilitator's story allows boys to then describe similar or related experiences that they would not have shared on their own. When boys hear stories from adults, they are given permission to share more of themselves.

The use of facilitator stories in BAM! groups makes us as leaders "walk the talk" about being the kind of person we are asking the boys to become. When we share of ourselves, we are modeling contact. We are providing an example of a person who has access to his own feelings and experience as well as the skills to express and converse about those feelings. It is particularly important for boys to witness these qualities in male leaders because many of these boys see so few examples of these characteristics in men. Through our use of strategic storytelling, we show that we are able and willing to share with the boys in ways that help the whole group grow more supportive of its members.

Strategic storytelling also serves to make abstract concepts more concrete, a benefit that is particularly important for preteen boys who don't yet have much ability to understand abstraction. The ability to make sense of the world through story and metaphor is one of the first cognitive capabilities that emerge in children (Bruner, 1990). Through story, we integrate our experiences in life with our feelings and thoughts about those experiences. In so doing, we open a door to making sense of abstract and complex concepts. For example, by listening to a story about what happens when a boy wears a pink shirt to school (see BAM! Example week 5 for more details), fifth-grade boys can begin to understand concepts like social pressure and gender identity that otherwise would stay meaninglessly abstract.

In short, the use of strategic storytelling in a school-age boys' group makes developmental sense because storytelling enhances contact, allows the leader to model the qualities we are asking the boys to learn, and helps the boys understand better the important themes of the group.

We've spoken about the rationale for leaders sharing personal stories, but what about the potential pitfalls of this method? The primary reason that most counseling programs discourage counselors from using personal stories is that such self-disclosure can blur the boundaries between the helper and client. In other words, the purpose of the helping relationship is to serve and support the client, not the counselor. If a counselor shares something of himself that elicits a caretaking response from the client, the boundaries are blurred and the counselor's effectiveness is compromised. In the most egregious examples, these unclear boundaries can lead to an abuse of power on the part of the counselor, with the helper using the relationship for his own gain.

To ensure that the stories we tell are in the best interest of the boys and do not compromise our effectiveness as leaders, we choose our stories carefully. We check with co-facilitators to ensure that the story meets the intentions behind strategic storytelling. We would not, for example, tell a story with the intention of receiving support from group members. Stories are told for the benefit of the group, not for the leader's benefit. We are careful that the stories we tell, for example, are emotionally resolved for us enough to avoid a situation in which one of the boys would feel the need to take care of us as leaders. One way to take the emotional charge out of a story is to have one leader tell the other leader's story. The stories we tell are brief, approximately 5 minutes long or less, so as not to take up too much group time.

What makes a good story? First, the story should be relevant to the topic and the age group of the participants. As leaders, we spend time brainstorming with each other lists of stories from our childhood that illustrate themes such as sticking up for others, challenges in family life, getting teased, being different, and so forth. We also make sure that our stories are supportive of the BAM! group objectives we outlined in the last section. Stories should therefore exemplify the social challenges boys face, illustrate success at overcoming those challenges, or endorse a broad range of emotions, to name a few examples. We are aware that storytelling in BAM! groups has unique challenges for women leaders, and we address these differences later in BAM! Instructions.

Storytelling is more effective when the stories are rich in detail. Before telling a story, picture the scene in your mind. What were the sights, sounds, and smells of the time? When you tell a story from your own experience we recommend you use names for the characters in the story, describe the settings, and recall the street names. Tell it as if it were happening now. The more you can be present in the telling, the more the boys will be present in their listening. Lean in toward the boys, use hand gestures, change the pace, the pitch, and the rhythm of your voice. Practice your story ahead of time to hear the parts of the story that are most powerful at creating contact. Notice when your listeners are giving you their best attention. Use humor and have fun!

The use of intentional facilitator self-disclosure is an effective method to help reach BAM! goals; yet it must be handled thoughtfully. Strategic storytelling is one of the two main methods employed in BAM! groups. The other is physical challenge, which we address next.

## Making Contact Through Physical Challenges

In addition to a facilitator story, each BAM! group session contains a group physical challenge. In this section we describe the rationale for using physical challenges, speak to the role that the facilitator plays in setting up and debriefing these activities, and discuss a few cautions.

As we have described previously, boys and men often depend on side-by-side, shared physical activities to strengthen their relationships, whereas girls and women more often strengthen bonds through face-to-face self-disclosure (Tannen, 1990). However, in their day-to-day experience, boys are often told to quiet down, be less active, and keep their hands to themselves. Sometimes these corrections are necessary and appropriate. At other times, however, these reprimands simply reflect adults' discomfort with boys' naturally high energy levels and send a disapproving message to boys. In BAM! groups we use physical activities to harness boys' inherent tendency toward action. We allow boys to be physically active and engaged without being shamed for it. However, we also use the physical challenges to provide the boys with guidance about how to skillfully manage and regulate their physicality in social contexts.

In addition to creating outlets for boys' energy and opportunities to guide their physicality, the activities used in BAM! groups create cohesion among group members, make abstract ideas more concrete, and build a playful learning atmosphere. By participating in activities with one another, boys build a sense of connection and belonging. In BAM! groups, participants must work cooperatively and supportively to complete the physical challenges, helping make the group environment inclusive and safe. Moreover, many of the initiatives rely on physical contact among group members to complete tasks. This physical contact also draws group members together. Over time, the completed physical challenges become a shared storehouse of memories for the boys. These shared memories help to further build group cohesion and identity.

In addition to creating cohesion among group members, the physical challenges in this guidebook are intended to make abstract ideas more concrete. Important BAM! concepts like trust, safety, and cooperation are brought to life and experienced physically. For example, during our first meeting with the boys, we speak with them about the need to work together and trust one another. We put these abstract concepts into action by having them imagine that they are all lost in the woods, that they are all hungry, and that they all need to work together to get the entire group over an "electric fence" in front of them in order to survive. After completing their mission, the boys are able to speak about how it felt to belong, to cooperate, and to trust.

The effectiveness of these activities is determined by the facilitator's ability to bring the challenges to life and to meaningfully debrief them. The more convincing the facilitator can be in telling the stories that set up the challenges, the more successful the activities will be. We have learned as facilitators that when we bring our full selves to the group in a committed and playful way, the boys are more likely to be fully present and engaged themselves.

Perhaps more important than the activities themselves is the way in which these activities are processed. In debriefing the activities, we intentionally orchestrate contact among group members, draw out lessons learned, and seize opportunities to illustrate BAM! goals. Activities can be debriefed in terms of insights gained individually, among a few of the boys, or as a whole group. For more ideas about setting up and debriefing these types of challenges the reader is referred to the following text: *Quicksilver: Adventure Games, Initiative Problems, Trust Activities and a Guide to Effective Leadership* by Steve Butler and Karl Rohnke (1995).

Safety is always the top priority when performing BAM! challenges. Facilitators must be vigilant in their efforts to create physical and emotional safety in the group. As we discuss later, vigilance involves preparation, the use of safety equipment, safety instruction for group members, and the facilitator's careful attention to group dynamics. The BAM! Instructions section details safety precautions for each activity.

In addition to the obvious safety issues around falling, for example, there are more subtle ones like the appropriate use of touch among group members and leaders. The daily news contains too many examples of adults' misuse of physical touch with children. As a result physical contact has become almost taboo in educational, mentoring, and counseling settings. And yet, most people recognize the value of even small amounts of appropriate physical contact to strengthen relationships and emotional well-being. In a clear and safe group environment, intentional and appropriate use of touch can increase contact. Just as leaders must be aware of the potential abuse of power through facilitator self-disclosure in strategic storytelling, they must be cognizant of the potential misuse of touch while also recognizing its value to help create contact. Again, the principle is to be conscious of the intentions behind the physical contact. The goal should be to increase connection among members and, at the same time, preserve a safe and comfortable group atmosphere.

Because the activities involve physical challenges, we believe that the boys should be able to determine the degree to which they participate. We call this "challenge by choice." If a boy feels unsafe participating in a given activity, he should be encouraged to clearly state his discomfort. By doing so, he is demonstrating an ability to check in with himself and stand firm for what he believes rather than to succumb to social pressure. This admission can be especially challenging for a boy if he finds that he is the only one who feels apprehensive about a particular activity. By determining the amount of exposure they are willing to take, the boys are able to practice self-care skills and rehearse for times when they may be pushed by peers to take other risks they aren't comfortable taking. Participants should be acknowledged when they care for themselves in this way. This moment may be a good entrée into discussion about social pressures outside of the group.

When a boy decides not to participate in a certain activity, we find some way to help him stay in contact with the group. Because one of the overarching themes of BAM! groups is to develop and maintain contact with others, we work to not let a boy isolate himself. We may assign him a different role, give him other opportunities for involvement, or one of the facilitators may make an effort to make a connection with him off to the side of the activity.

It is a joy to see a group of boys in a setting where they are free to let down their guard and to be natural with one another. The physical challenges are fun and help to establish a more natural environment for the boys. Creating safe places for boys by understanding and utilizing their styles of communication helps to establish a climate in which boys feel free to be authentic.

In the next section of this guidebook, BAM! Example, we provide a detailed narrative example of a 10-week group for boys in which we used both strategic storytelling and physical challenges with the boys in our care. Following the BAM! Example section is a section entitled BAM! Instructions, in which we provide careful step-by-step instructions on how you can lead your own group through this same 10-week sequence.

# BAM! Example

## Week 1: Lost in the Woods

"Cool," one of the boys says as he files into the room for our first group meeting, "how do you draw like that?" He is commenting on a butcher-paper poster that Peter is making on the floor. The poster reads, in big block letters, "FIFTH-GRADE BOYS BAM! GROUP," and is being decorated with lots of colors. Before long, all nine boys have arrived (two more will join us next week) and have found a place to sit on one of the beanbag cubes that circle the small room. There is an easy chatter as they munch on the lunches they have brought with them and as they notice other boys they know in the group. We as leaders smile at each boy as he comes in and try to put a name to each face we see. In a few minutes, we will begin a name game using the colorful poster lying on the floor, but for now the poster serves the purpose of metaphorically "drawing the boys around the fire."

When all nine boys and all three leaders have assembled and found seats, Stephen begins by welcoming everyone. Because he works as a school counselor at Meadow Elementary School where our meetings are being held (we use a fictional name for the school, as we do for all the names of the boys mentioned in this narrative), he knows and has recruited each of the boys that surround us now. Many of the boys know about the boys groups that have been offered in years past and were eager to join this time around. Some of the other boys have been recommended by their teacher or by the principal for various reasons. A few of the boys struggle with making and keeping friends, others have had very difficult home lives, and all of them can benefit from feeling a sense of belonging to a supportive group of peers.

"This is the fifth year we are offering boys groups at Meadow," Stephen says in his introduction, "because we think that boys at your age are learning to be really competitive and aggressive with each other, but that you don't really get a chance to be supportive and cooperative together. Boys learn early in life to use put-downs and act like they don't care about a lot of important things, but here in this group we want to give you a chance to practice making friends and being part of a team that works together, faces challenges, and has fun. How does that sound?" Most of the boys nod their heads in silent agreement after Stephen speaks and then listen attentively as Howard begins to speak:

> I want us to play a name game so we all can remember each other's names. I want you to come up with a nickname for yourself and Peter will write it down on the poster for us to remember you by. So I'll go first, I'll be Helpin' Howard because I'm a counselor and I like to help people.

Some of the boys know immediately what they want to be called, but some of the other boys get stuck trying to come up with a nickname. In these cases, some of the other boys try to offer nicknames to one another, and some of the better ones stick. In other cases, though, the nicknames offered are rejected. Edward, for example, rejects Easy Edward and instead chooses Edward Elephant—which is interesting because Edward is originally from India, having been adopted by parents in the United States. After each boy comes up with his nickname, Howard leads the boys in a double clap, followed by the group stating aloud each boy's name and nickname (e.g., clap, clap, "Helpin' Howard"!). A constellation of all the boys' names and nicknames eventually appears around the edge of the poster:

> Crazy Curtis
> Cool Keith
> Edward Elephant
> Dirtbikin' Drake
> JoJo Jesus
> Sleepin' Sorin
> Theo Thundergod
> Juvenile James
> Ice Skatin' Isaiah

We as adult leaders also pick a name for ourselves, following Howard's lead. Stephen becomes Skateboardin' Stephen and Peter becomes Guitar Pickin' Peter. After the name game is complete, Howard states: "I want to tell you a story about when I was in fifth grade. . . ." This statement catches the boys' attention, and they listen as he continues:

> I was about 10 years old. I was always a poor athlete, a little slow, husky, and uncoordinated. I struck out most times at bat in little league. Mostly kids liked me anyway because I was a good team supporter.
>
> One time we were playing at the field at Sharp Corners School, and I came up to bat and swung and I hit the ball but nobody could find it! My coach started yelling, "Run, Howie, run!" I got to first base and paused while the outfielders, infielders, and the other team's coaches were looking around for the ball. Still no ball! Each base I got to . . . 2nd, 3rd.

The same thing! I would pause, but still there was no ball! Now the fans were yelling at me to keep running. Everyone was involved. Eventually, they waved me home and I scored. Moments later, the opposing coach found the ball lodged underneath the catcher's chest protector where it landed after my foul tip!

I remember having a mix of feelings that day. I was happy that I scored, but I was also sort of humiliated that it had happened that way. Still, everyone got a good laugh out of it. I wanted to tell you this story because I know not all of you are great athletes, and I wanted you to know that I wasn't a great athlete either. But I did have a sense of humor and kids liked me for that. What I imagine is that each of you has special strengths and talents that we will get to see as our group goes on over the next few weeks.

After Howard completes his story, Stephen begins his own personal story to introduce himself to the group. By this time, the boys are fully engaged in what is happening. They shift their attention from Howard to Stephen and listen quietly while they munch on their sandwiches, some with slightly slack jaws as they listen. Story time for fifth graders. Stephen begins:

I grew up in New York. In the fifth grade, I played on a Little League team. Lots of my friends were on my team, the Tigers. But my friend Jeffrey Ferrara played on another team, the Lions. He was their pitcher and the Lions were the best team in the league. Jeffrey was very athletic but a little shy. He was a great pitcher.

One day, we had a game against the Lions, and Jeffrey was pitching. For some reason, Jeffrey was not having a good day at the mound, and we were hitting a lot of his pitches. It was clear that Jeffrey was shaken by all the hits, and my team decided to take advantage of this. They started chanting, "We want a pit-cher, not a belly-itcher!" If Jeffrey was rattled before, he was completely shaken up now. He was looking more and more like he might cry as my teammates yelled louder and louder, "We want a pit-cher, not a belly-itcher!"

Because Jeffrey was my friend, I felt really bad for him. I wanted to win the game but not at the expense of my friend's humiliation. When I couldn't watch or listen any more, I stood up on the bench behind my teammates and yelled, "Leave him alone! That's enough you guys! That's enough!" My teammates and coach looked at me like I was crazy, but they stopped chanting.

That was my last season playing organized sports, but Jeffrey remained my friend. Many years later, when we were talking about this story, my stepfather, who was watching the game, said to me, "At that moment, I knew that you would never be a professional ballplayer."

I think I told you this story because it says a little bit about the conflicts that I faced as a boy and that I think most boys face. They want to be friends with each other, but sometimes they are almost forced to be mean to each other. In this group, I hope we can face some challenges together as a team and also be friends with each other afterward.

When Stephen finishes his story, Peter tells the boys that he is not going to tell a story of his own this week, but that he will have one for next week. "No! Come on, tell your story now!" said Edward, one of the boys who has been described to us by his mother as immature. Peter is touched that Edward would want to hear his story. He also realizes at this moment that we as adult leaders have managed to hook the boys with our personal stories. In the weeks to come, our storytelling will continue to be a powerful tool we will use to make personal contact with the boys and also to convey many of the ideas we wish the boys to learn. This is the use of stories to convey curriculum.

Instead of telling a story, Peter tells the boys a little bit more about the history of the boys groups at Meadow Elementary School. He describes how, for the past 5 years, one of the goals of the boys groups has been to work toward a special event at the end of the 2 months that is an exciting final challenge for the boys. He goes on to say:

> Two years ago, we took the boys on a final, full-day adventure involving canoes and a trip across the Willamette River to Ross Island. We had a picnic, we had rock-throwing contests, we looked for eagles, and we had a treasure hunt using compasses. However, on the way back from that big adventure on the island, one of the canoes tipped over and three of the boys ended up in the water. They were all wearing life jackets, of course, but the rest of the boys really had to work together as a team to help everyone safely to shore. We all made it back in one piece, and it was actually a really good way to see how far we had come as a group and how much we were able to work together as a team.

In telling this story, Peter wants to elicit in the boys a sense of excitement as well as a sense of seriousness about the challenge of building a strong group together. Peter next tells the boys, "We have a challenge for you to participate in right now." The boys, finished with their lunches and by now excited to move, jump to their feet and stand against one of the walls as Peter hushes them into silence and tells them the following imagined scenario:

> You are all lost in the woods! You have been lost for 3 days without any food other than the grubs you have found under logs and you have had no water except for the dew you have collected from leaves in the morning. You are hungry and thirsty and you each have 5 bucks in your pockets that you would love to spend on a hamburger and a milkshake somewhere.
>
> Suddenly, after 3 long days, you come to the edge of the forest and there it is! Right across the meadow is a Burgerville! You rush to get to it, but one of you jumps back with a shriek after getting shocked by an electric fence that stands between you and your first burger all week!
>
> Your challenge as a group is the following: You must get everyone in your group safely over this electric fence [Peter points to a piece of red

yarn we have tied about 4 feet off the ground, stretching over a 2-inch-thick gym mat]. There are a few rules: You many not touch or go under the fence and you may not throw anyone over the fence. In fact, you must stay in physical contact with the person going over the fence at all times. Be gentle.

Oh look! Here are three kindly farmers to help you on this side of the fence [Peter points to himself, Stephen, and Howard, all with big smiles on their faces and arms outstretched to help them on their crossing]. Now take a few moments to plan amongst yourselves how you will get everyone over the fence safely before you attempt this dangerous crossing.

The boys excitedly begin throwing out ideas to one another. James almost immediately suggests, "Let's have someone big get down on their knees as a stepladder for the rest of us." Theo adds, "But we all have to take off our shoes first!" We as leaders are watching carefully to see this first example of group dynamics at work: Who emerges as a leader? Who stays quiet? Who has good ideas but is not listened to? Before long, one boy at a time is stepping gently onto the back of another and being helped over the "electric fence" by the group of boys and adults, all working together. There is much excitement, and, as more boys gather on the far side of the fence, the leaders back off and let the boys help each other on both sides of the fence.

When everyone has completed the task (an adult "farmer" has miraculously appeared on the boys' side of the fence to help the last boy over), enough time remains in the first hour session to ask the boys what they experienced in this first activity. Sorin comments seriously that he "really had to trust everyone." Drake seconds that thought, stating, "It was little bit scary but everyone was really helping."

Howard mentions in closing that today the boys showed that they could both listen attentively as well as act in supportive ways with one another. "We only have four main rules for this group," he states. "Be respectful; listen to learn; take risks but be safe; and keep confidentiality." Stephen asks how many of the boys would like to come back next week and be willing to follow these rules. They all raise their hands. Stephen says he is glad and asks them to show him they can act respectfully by walking quietly and calmly back to their classrooms.

## Week 2: Alligator Swamp

During the process of screening boys to join this year's group at Meadow Elementary School, Stephen spoke with the parents of each prospective boy to help them understand our goals for the group and what their son might gain from the experience of being in the group. Most parents were enthusiastic about the opportunity for their sons to be part of such a group, but one parent's comments stood out for us as emblematic of a concern we have faced over the years in offering these boys groups. Isaiah's mom told Stephen that she was happy to have her son join the group, but, she added, "My husband has a concern." When Stephen asked her to say more about the concern, Isaiah's mom responded that her husband "didn't want Isaiah to join a group that would make him gay."

In our following discussions with Stephen about this comment, we as group leaders noted how difficult it was to clearly communicate what we were trying to accomplish in our boys groups. We also noted a connection between our work with boys and the early days of the women's liberation movement when the fight for a broader personal and professional repertoire for women increased fears in some that women would become "just like men." We noted these similarities between the women's movement and our fledgling "young men's movement," but we also noted a significant difference. While there is some status gained for women taking on roles and identities traditionally related to the world of men (everything from wearing pants to being stronger physically), the opposite is not always the case. In many ways it is cool to be a "tomboy," but what is the equivalent for boys? There is not as much to be gained for a young man to take on the attributes that have traditionally been aligned with what it means to be a female in our culture. So how do we help boys gain such skills without them thinking they are giving up something central to their essential maleness? How do we help the boys we work with (and their parents) expand their acceptable definitions of what it means to be male and see it as a positive thing?

We as leaders take a stand on these core issues related to our boys groups and we communicate this as openly as possible. We tell the boys and their parents that every boy is different, that every boy brings varying strengths and skills to our group, and that all boys will be accepted and tolerated in our group, as long as they work to accept and tolerate others who may be different from them. We are also openly supportive of a wide range of possible male identities and qualities—strong is good, sensitive is too—and although we don't discuss sexuality openly in our groups, we do confront prejudice and homophobia when they arise because we believe these issues are at the heart of what keeps boys and men constrained to narrow and unhealthy definitions of masculinity.

On the day of our second meeting of the boys group, a new member's arrival allowed us all to test our tolerance and acceptance. Paul arrived with a handful of the boys from his class, looked around at the numerous beanbag cubes circling the room, and immediately declared, "I want the pink one, I'm feeling especially pink today!" All the boys in the group know Paul even if he is not in their class. He is an articulate, expressive, and vivid presence, especially in comparison with most other fifth-grade boys. Paul regularly attends after-school drama classes, is an active member of the local ballet organization, and has a couple of long braids of hair with beads tied into them.

As Peter is signing in the boys for this second group meeting by putting a star next to each boy's name on the poster, which is once again spread out on the floor in the center of the room, he asks Paul to think of a nickname for himself. Paul thinks it over for a minute and then states confidently, "I'm Peacock Paul!" This statement is immediately followed by a comment made by Theo under his breath that was too quiet for everyone but Howard to pick up on. Howard reported to us later that Theo mumbled, "Maybe you should have picked pink instead." As we will show in later chapters of this narrative account, Peacock Paul's presence in our group will richly aid our quest to help the boys broaden their acceptance and tolerance of what it means to be a boy.

Another new boy on this second week of our group is a heavy-set 10-year-old who introduces himself as Enthusiastic Enrique, although he is very shy and struggles with the English language. We will find out later that Enrique was born in Mexico, lived in California most of his life, and has only recently moved to this city and school. With all 11 members of our group present, and after Peter has taken roll, Stephen begins by greeting the boys and reminding each of them of the rules Howard had described during our first meeting. He states:

> We want this group to be a fun and a safe place where we can do interesting things together. So we all need to work to be honest, to take some risks, to listen attentively to each other, to respect each other and ourselves, and to not blab what we talk about in our group all over the school. We want you guys to know you can talk about things here without being afraid someone is going to laugh at you or spread gossip all over the place. This week we have some cool activities planned for you, but first, because there were some requests last week, we want Peter to have a chance to tell you his story. So we are going to start with that.

As the boys settle down to eat their lunches quietly, Peter begins to relate his story:

> In some ways, I was similar to Howard when I was younger. Howard talked about striking out in baseball a lot. I used to strike out so much in the fifth grade that the boys in my class called me the "strikeout king" for a while. Then one day during a big game with a neighboring school, I really connected with the ball. I really smacked it and it felt good. I watched the ball curve high over the third baseman's head and land right on the chalk foul line in deep left field. I remember seeing how it sent up a plume of white chalk dust when it hit. I started running the bases hard. I was so excited!

It wasn't until after I had rounded first base and was on my way to second base that I heard the umpire yelling "Foul ball!" and the boys on the other team were telling me to stop running. When I heard the umpire, I immediately started crying in front of everyone because it felt so unfair that the ball had been called foul. I felt like I had been robbed! I felt really angry at the umpire, and I also felt embarrassed that I was crying in front of all the boys on both teams. I guess I was an emotional kid.

After Peter finishes his story, he pauses and there is a moment of silence in the group. "I'm that way, too," Colin finally says quietly but loud enough for everyone to hear. "So am I," says Paul. For a few minutes after Peter's story, the boys talk avidly about what it is like to face fastballs thrown your way "at 35 miles an hour" as well as what it is like to get hit by a baseball, how scary it is, and how much it hurts. When the boys have quieted down a bit, Howard mentions that he thinks Peter's story is about how boys can have a range of feelings when something like that happens—from sadness, to anger, to embarrassment—and how sometimes you can even have all those feelings at once. Howard says:

> We will be talking a lot about feelings in this group, what it's like to have them and what you do with them once you have them. But for right now, we are going to switch to hearing stories from you. We are going to do an activity called the 60-Second Autobiography and it goes like this: Every boy in this room will get a chance to tell his life story in only 60 seconds, though we might not get through everyone today. You don't have a lot of time to tell your story, so I'm going to be watching the clock and I will tell you when your time is up. Then, after each of you is done telling your story, I'm going to ask the boy on your left and the boy on your right to say one thing that they learned about you by listening carefully to your story. If you already know the boy sitting next to you, listen carefully because I am sure you will learn something new about him. Okay, who wants to start?

Although as a group we only get through about half of the boys and their 60-Second Autobiographies (surprisingly, some of the boys need prompting to fill up a minute's worth of time), there is a clear theme that emerges from this day's stories regarding divorce and complex family arrangements. At the end of the six stories that the group hears, Peter asks, "Did you all notice anything similar that each of you share in your lives?" Drake responds sardonically, "Yeah. We're all divorced." By asking this question, Peter tries to address one of the main goals of the group: to help the boys to know that they are not alone in many of the experiences and emotions they will bring to the group. In past years, one of our greatest and most surprising discoveries was to find out how lonely the boys felt before they had joined the group and how many more friends they felt they had and could count on by the time the group had ended. We as leaders strive to help boys in the group connect not only to themselves and their own emotional life, but also to the experiences of others in the group. One of the main things we want them to take away from the group, in short, is that being a boy does not have to mean feeling alone.

With about 20 minutes left in the group for the day, Stephen mentions that we have one more activity planned for the boys, a physical challenge. "We can't just sit here all day," says Stephen as he stands up, expecting the boys to be anxious to move after all the good listening they have been doing. "Why not?" asks James, looking content to sit and continue listening. His comment lets us know that we are on the right track. We have begun to create a place that is both safe and comfortable for the boys to inhabit each week. Given the boys' often contentious experiences on the playgrounds each day (dealing with arguments, challenges, and often feelings of being isolated or singled out), we know that the group may be an all-too-rare experience for them.

The boys scramble to their feet when Stephen tells them with enthusiasm that the activity is called the Alligator Swamp. He goes on to tell them, "It's all about working together as a group and paying close attention to what others can teach you." The boys begin on one end of the room and must negotiate their way through the swamp by stepping on alligator heads in exactly the right order (the alligator heads, in this case, are simply pieces of masking tape on the floor). As the boys line up and begin to take on this challenge, the room is quiet but filled with excitement and much pointing. One by one, the boys pick out more of the correct steps they need to take until finally Keith makes it all the way through to the end of the "swamp" safely. Spontaneously, Peter picks Keith up by the armpits as he exits the maze and puts him down in front of Howard who picks him up again and puts him down in the corner of the room. Soon, all the boys are making their way through the maze and approaching Peter at the end, also expecting to be lifted up. In this moment, a group ritual is born.

Interestingly, as Peacock Paul makes his way through the maze, he performs ballet leaps and jumps, ending with a flourish. Nobody makes any critical comments on Paul's dancing, and everyone looks pleased with the success of the group in facing this challenge together. Before the boys leave, Howard asks everyone to sit down briefly so we can talk about what we have accomplished together. He acknowledges the boys for working well as a group to figure out the swamp and says that he can already see improvement in the way that everyone is working together from the first week to this second meeting. He also mentions that one challenge he noticed for many of the boys was how hard it was to slow down and be thoughtful before jumping ahead in the maze. Often this jumping ahead ended up in mistakes being made, Howard notes. He describes how he thinks many boys face this challenge in schools: "We will be paying attention to learning more about slowing down and being mindful," he states.

For a few minutes at the end of the group, the boys openly share about times they have each struggled with "doing before thinking." Drake tells how he got so frustrated with his younger brother last week that he hit him. Edward describes how some other boys dared him to steal someone else's lunch and he did. There is no bravado as the boys tell these tales. Their hushed tones and embarrassed glances tell us how badly they feel about their actions. In order to give them practice in being more mindful, Stephen tells the boys that their homework is to report back next week with one thing they *didn't* do because they thought about it first. The boys, looking content and connected after only this second week as a group, head quietly back to class.

## Week 3: Haunted House

As the boys walked out of our second meeting, a few boys talked about costumes and one of them said, "Next week in boys group, let's do something for Halloween." We took this idea and ran with it. As the boys approach the counseling office on this day of our third meeting—the day before Halloween—they have no idea what we have in store for them. They laugh and joke as they pass kindergarteners showing off their costumes—little dinosaurs, petite fairy princesses, and miniature Spidermen. Perhaps our fifth graders assume we have some candy treats waiting for them or a game involving bobbing for apples. Instead, after we get started with a few more of them telling us their 60-Second Autobiographies, Stephen asks them to quiet down and listen up because he has something important to tell them about a problem at the school. With a serious tone, he says:

> I need to tell you guys that there is something in the basement of this school. It has been there all week. Yesterday one of the staff went down to solve the problem and he hasn't come back yet. Some people heard a few loud screams and there are weird electrical problems happening all over the school. We weren't going to tell you about it, none of the other kids at school know, but the principal asked us to talk to you as a group. Yesterday at the faculty meeting, the principal asked if anyone could come up with any ideas on what to do about the thing in the basement. Someone mentioned it might be a good job for the fifth-grade boys group. We think you guys are ready for this challenge, but it's not going to be easy.

A quick look around the room as he pauses tells Stephen that even though most of the boys have smirked at least once during his telling of this tall tale, he has them where he wants them: They are listening intently with only occasional bursts of nervous laughter. He continues:

> Here's what we know. We know this thing can kill you if you look at it directly. We also know that you will die if it finds you alone. So here's the plan: We are going to need to blindfold each of you so you can't see the monster. But you can hold on to the arm of the boy in front of you. In fact you will need to hold on to him if you want to survive. Remember, if it finds you alone, it's all over for you. We also know that this thing will be chased off if we use a particular chant that seems to have worked at other schools. We will lead you all the way down into the basement and there you will have to perform the chant perfectly. Peter will show you how to do the chant now.

Peter tells the boys to each put one hand into the center of the circle and he then leads them through a sports team-like chant that starts with the boys making a low and quiet sound together and ends up in a loud and high shout as their arms go up. We as leaders then spend a few minutes getting the boys blindfolded and ready to go. At this point, they are a little worked up by the story and the blindfolds, but they are eager to be part of this fun but also slightly scary challenge.

We lead the boys into the hallway of the school, hush them into silence as they pass other classrooms and help them on their way down the stairs. The boys stumble a bit with their blindfolds on, but they each hold tight to the shoulder of the boy in front of them. By the time they get down into the basement, where there are noisy machines and tight corners, the boys have passed a gauntlet of scary stuff. They have been told to be careful not to step on the dead animals that the monster has left behind (baseball gloves strewn over the floor) and to pay no attention to the skulls falling at their feet (softballs that bounce down the stairs in front of them). They have also been repeatedly reminded not to take off their blindfolds and not to lose physical contact with each other. Bats fly around their heads (crossing-guard banners shaken at close proximity), and Stephen and Howard occasionally let out howls and shrieks that add to the general sense of danger and gloom.

Eventually, the boys all make it to the monster's room (the boiler room). They can tell it's the monster's room by the loud howling (provided by Stephen) as well as the loud hissing (the boiler). All of them get together to successfully do the chant they have practiced, yelling loudly at the end to exorcise the monster who leaves with a banging of doors before the boys can take off their blindfolds. Soon, they are happily making their way back to the counseling room, talking excitedly about their Halloween adventure.

Back in the room, Howard asks them to talk about what they experienced. The boys go around telling what they had physically encountered (the noises, the skulls, the dead cats), but no one mentions anything about his internal experiences (feelings of excitement or fear, worries about getting lost or cut off from the group, etc.).

To us, this is a stark contrast to what happened when we led the previous boys group through a similar experience last year at Halloween. Even before we finished blindfolding some of the boys that year, we found two boys with their heads down, quietly sniffling back tears because they were so scared. At that point, we realized we may have overdone it a bit. But those tears shed by those boys opened the gates to discussions about how it's okay for boys to have all kinds of feelings. We had used those tears as an opportunity to appreciate the ones who had cried for being brave enough to be vulnerable, for helping everyone else in the group know that all kinds of feelings could be felt and expressed here. One of the boys who had cried at Halloween also cried after the winter break when he told us that his house had burned down over the holiday. By that time, there was no question that tears would be allowed in the group.

Had we made this year's challenge too easy so as not to scare the boys too much? We wondered this as the group talked and joked about what they had experienced this year in the basement, staying at a superficial level in their conversations. For example, Theo said: "I knew the whole thing was fake. It didn't scare me at all."

Then, just toward the end of our processing time, Drake mentions that Curtis hasn't said anything yet. All eyes turned to Curtis, one of the quieter boys in the group, as he took a moment to collect his thoughts. "In the basement," he finally said, looking down, "I was cut off for a while and it was kinda sc--." Before he finishes this sentence he falters and stops, not saying the word that would admit his vulnerability to the group of boys for whom, today, that was clearly a taboo topic. Howard asks him to finish what it was he was going to say, and, at that point, Curtis admits that he was "kinda scared" during the basement challenge when he thought he had lost contact with the others in the group. When Curtis has finished, Howard says that he appreciates him for being honest about what he had felt. Howard then raises his own hand and asks, "How many of you would be willing to admit that at some point in the basement challenge you felt at least a little bit scared?" Nearly all the boys raise a hand and suddenly the conversation shifts. Edward admits that he was afraid that "the monsters were gonna get me." Another boy somewhat seriously jokes, "Tonight I'm gonna have nightmares."

In the last few minutes of this third session, Stephen again acknowledges Curtis for being the first one in the group to honestly talk about the fear he had felt in the basement. Stephen also takes a moment to appreciate Drake for what he had told the group in his 60-Second Autobiography. During his 1-minute introduction of himself at the beginning of today's group, Drake had told the everyone that he had undergone two serious operations when he was a younger boy and that those operations had left him with still-noticeable scars on his back and neck. Stephen tells Drake that he thinks Drake is a strong boy for admitting that there is something not perfect about him. As is typical in many counseling situations, with literally just a minute to go before we have to send the boys back to their classes, Drake tags on one more thing after Stephen finishes appreciating him. Drake says, "Yeah, and another thing is that my mom went away from me when I was 3 years old and I haven't seen her since. . . ."

Stephen acknowledges Drake's sad comment without going further into it, telling the group that our family situations will be a good thing to continue talking about next week.

## Week 4: Sitting Circle

On the day of our fourth meeting, everyone shows up right on time. All 11 boys are back and there is a general loose chatter and easy rapport while some eat their lunches and others munch on snacks. Jesus again has a full can of "red hot" potato chips, as he does every week. These chips garner a lot of attention and discussion. As a result there is quite a bit of food bartering that happens at the outset of the meeting: a handful of chips for a couple of cookies, and so forth. Peter teases Jesus about the fat content in a whole can of potato chips and then eats a few himself. Howard begins the group by saying, "This is amazing attendance, you guys are all here this week. Nice."

Stephen takes a moment to summarize what had happened last week in our group for the two boys who had missed it. He reviews the Haunted House activity, the disclosure of vulnerable feelings like being scared, and how important it was that some boys were able to take the risk of being honest in the group: "The haunted house was fake, you guys, but the feelings you had weren't." In reference to Drake's disclosure in last week's group about his mom leaving him at an early age, Stephen wraps up his summary by saying that this week we will be spending some time talking about our families as a way to get to know one another better.

Howard then chimes in to remind us all about the rules of the group. He says:

> Remember, we agreed that this group would be about both having fun and being safe, both physically and emotionally. We also agreed to be honest in what we say, to take some risks, and to listen to each other with the intention of learning from each other. We also agreed to respect ourselves and each other and to have confidentiality outside of the group. We talked about how confidentiality means having the confidence that you can say things in this group and other boys won't blab it around the school.

Continuing our theme of narrative disclosure from the leaders, Stephen next says that he would like to tell the boys a story about growing up and what he learned—and what he didn't learn—from his family:

> I want to tell you guys a story about what I learned with my family. My dad didn't take good care of himself. He had a stressful job where he dealt with lots of racism. So when he got home from work, he drank lots of alcohol, smoked, and ate food that wasn't good for him. He worked hard and loved us, but he ended up getting very sick and he eventually died from a stroke. That happened when I was only one and a half, so I did not get to spend much time with my father, but I learned quite a bit from him. My father worked hard, and he was able to get an education and a good job at a time when bad schools for black people and racism made it difficult for black men to be successful. I am proud of his

accomplishments, and I am reminded of how believing in yourself and not giving up can help you to achieve huge goals.

I also learned from my father about how men have a hard time dealing with their feelings. Instead of sharing his feelings with my mom, my father kept them inside, using alcohol to try to keep the feelings away. The result was that my father passed away far too early, leaving my brother and me to learn the hard way about how important it is for a man to deal with difficult feelings in positive ways. We were raised instead by our mother and grandmother. They did a great job of teaching us about what it means to be men. Now that I have my own children, I want to take better care of myself than my dad did of himself so that I can be around for my two boys as they grow up.

With this story and self-disclosure, Stephen is laying the groundwork for the boys to tell their own stories about their own families. We already know that many of the boys have stories that are not far removed from Stephen's experience.

After telling his story, Stephen hands the green "talking pen" (each week the talking object tends to end up being whatever is closest at hand) over to first Theo, then Enrique, and then James so they can finish their 60-Second Autobiographies. Theo builds on some of the themes from Stephen's story by talking a bit about how his own parents are divorced and how he doesn't get to see his dad very often because he lives in another state. Theo also talks about how he, like Stephen, hangs out with women and girls a lot and is more comfortable with them sometimes ("I know. Me too," adds James). Enrique tells about coming from Mexico and living in California for a few years before moving to Oregon. There is an almost audible hush in the room as Enrique, a normally very quiet presence in the group, tells his story. After Enrique's 60 seconds are over, Peter calls attention to Enrique's quiet presence by stating:

> I want you guys to notice something. Sometimes there are people in a group that like to talk a lot and sometimes there are people who are really quiet. It may be easy to overlook the quiet people in the group. But I have noticed that when someone like Enrique, who is usually quiet, speaks in a group, everyone is really interested in him and listens really carefully, just like you all just did. That tells me that sometimes, quiet people in a group have a lot of power and are really interesting, too.

Enrique smiles a bit bashfully but seems to enjoy being noticed in this way by Peter, and some of the other boys look at Enrique—to make contact with him—in a new way after Peter is done talking. Next, it is James's turn to take the "talking pen," and he tells the group, among other things in his 60 seconds, that his mom "has a drinking problem and so now I live with my dad and I haven't seen my mom in a long time." James is wearing a hooded sweatshirt. After he finishes speaking, he pulls the hood over his head so that much of his face is obscured. He then leans back against the wall, perhaps withdrawing a bit after this much disclosure on his part. Within moments, though, Drake asks for the "talking pen" from James and tells the group, "I'm a little like James. My mom has a drinking problem, too, and I got traded to my dad last year."

Edward then asks for the talking pen and tells the group, all of whom are quietly engaged and listening attentively, that he was adopted from India and that his dad died too long ago for him to remember. "Are you an orphan?" Drake quietly asks. "I was," says Edward.

After this sharing and conversation has subsided for few moments, Howard acknowledges Drake for having said that he was "a little like James." Howard goes on to say:

> Boys often feel that they experience things that they can't share with anyone else. So I appreciate when Drake said that he was "a little like James" because it shows that James is not alone in having a tough experience with his family. I also want to reinforce the idea that this group has agreed to confidentiality. Let's put our hands together if we agree with that . . . like the chant we did to release the demon in the basement.

With this prompt, each boy puts a hand in the center of the circle and the whole group lets out a holler. Peter then asks the boys to circle up and leads them through a Sitting Circle activity instead of the planned Willow in the Wind activity. The Sitting Circle activity will take less time. The boys eventually get the Sitting Circle activity right and sit for a few seconds suspended on only one anothers' laps in a circle before tumbling to the mat in a playful mess. It turns out to be a light, fun, and ultimately successful way for the boys to end this somewhat serious meeting. Even though there has been much sharing of difficult experiences in the group, the session ends on a positive note. Not only have the boys had the opportunity to make rich contact with one another emotionally on this day, they have also ended the hour in playful, physical contact, leaving them looking cheerful, connected, and relaxed.

# Week 5: Willow in the Wind

Because of the Thanksgiving holiday break and parent conferences being held at the school, it has been 3 weeks since we have convened by the time the boys ramble in for our fifth meeting. As we have come to expect, even after a 3-week absence, all 11 boys are in attendance on this rainy December day, and they have all shown up right on time. This is a good sign.

To start things off, Peter tells the boys he would like to hear a few words from each of them to see how everyone is doing. "So let's do this," he says, "If you were a weather system, what kind of weather system would you be today that would match your feelings? Calm? Stormy? I'll go first to show you what I mean. I think I would be a bit foggy today, but with a chance of sun breaks later on. I'm feeling a bit foggy this morning."

As the boys check in, some of the metaphors seem to accurately describe the emotional state of the boy ("I'd be a little rainy today," says Enrique, his face looking a little downcast), while other metaphors seem to be more an expression of a fantasy ("I'd be like this massive storm system or maybe a gadjillion degrees of heat!" says Theo, one of the biggest and most influential boys in the group). In either case, the metaphor certainly speaks to something about the boy who came up with it.

When we have gone around and heard a little bit from each of the boys, Stephen says he would like to tell them a story from his own life while they are finishing their lunches. He goes on to tell them about one particular day when he was living in New York:

> I went to junior high in the mid-80s in Brooklyn. In the seventh grade, I had one shirt that I was particularly fond of, a pink polo shirt that I wore with the collar turned up. This pink shirt became the excuse for a group of boys to pick a fight with me.
>
> Anthony Grazzle started it. I think he did it because he was the smallest guy in his group and he needed to "prove himself." He walked up to me in gym class and called me gay for wearing the pink shirt.
>
> I didn't hit Anthony, but I stood up and got in his face. Then he hit me and I hit him back. Before I knew it, a group of his friends were holding me while Anthony punched and kicked me. I still can't believe that the P.E. teacher never saw what happened. Everyone knew that an unresolved fight would be settled "after school." In fact, I think Anthony said those very words to me as we were separating.
>
> A crowd gathered after school, expecting to relocate to a place that was far enough away to not get caught by adults. I was really nervous and thought seriously about going home, but I was almost more afraid of what might happen if I did not show up. I worried that people would think I was chicken, and that other boys would pick on me even more. Feeling like I had no choice, I went to face Anthony hoping that at least one of my friends would tell me that they would still respect me if I did not go, maybe respect me more. I did not receive this support.

I learned a few things from that experience: I learned about being teased. I learned about how boys sometimes feel as though they have to stick up for themselves, being pushed to fight even when they don't want to. I learned that it is not always easy to be a boy. That it feels sometimes like you have to do things that you don't want to do in order for people to like and respect you.

Now I want to be very clear. I am not saying that I think that boys should fight in order to be accepted by their friends. I don't want you to fight at all. What I want is for you to know that the adults in this room understand how scary it can be to choose not to fight, how the fear that losing friends or getting picked on even more is real. Our hope, though, is that you will see that there are friends out there, like the ones that you have in this group, who will support you in staying out of fights, and who will not tease you for being different.

All the boys listen closely as Stephen tells his story. By now it has become customary in the group for the boys to listen attentively to a story told by one of us leaders, to reflect on it, and then to talk about it. We had thought carefully in advance about the kind of story we wanted to tell on this day. Our intention was to choose a story from our own experience of boyhood that would lead the boys to talk about teasing. We wanted to focus on teasing because we see it as being central to issues of power as well as gender development for the boys, of what they can and can't be.

After the boys have had a few moments to share a few stories of their own about being pushed into a fight and, in one case, about having to run away from certain aggressors, Peter asks them outright: "So we are interested in the part of Stephen's story where he got teased not only for wearing a pink shirt, but also for playing with his white friends. We want to make a list here on this big piece of paper of the things you get teased for. What are they?"

After a short pause, it is Enrique who speaks up first. Interestingly, Enrique has been one of the quieter members of the group. He is also the heaviest boy in the group. He says quietly that he is often teased for "being slow and being overweight." It doesn't take long before the following list is compiled with at least one contribution from each of the 11 boys:

> "Other boys give me nicknames I don't like"
> "I get teased for wearing bright colors, like orange"
> "I've been teased for having a weak stomach"
> "For being weak"
> "For being mentally slow"
> "I get teased for flinching when they flick fingers in my face"
> "For being bad at sports"
> "They tease me for having close friendships with boys"
> "For being gay"
> "For doing ballet and wearing a leotard"
> "I get teased for hanging out with girls too much"
> "I've been teased for being really light and small"

"I have weak bones"

"I've been teased for being too smart"

"For being with a guy who is being teased, like when I'm with Paul"

"I've been teased hard for making mistakes in sports"

The boys report getting teased for perceived weaknesses (stomach, strength, bones, being light and small, flinching); their bodies (small, fat, what you can wear, slowness, lack of skills or strength); and about lacking masculinity or being gay (wearing bright colors or leotards, having close friendships, doing ballet). None of these is a surprise to us. But still it is a solemn moment in the group when all these themes have all been spoken and written down. Being a boy, it is clear, is not an easy undertaking.

Howard thanks the boys for being willing to talk about these things and also notes that it must feel safe enough in this particular group to say these things without being teased. He tells the boys that we are going to work with this list some more next week. Isaiah pipes up at this point and asks if we are going to "do a challenge." Howard says that one of the challenges for this session was just to make this list, but that "Yes, we have a group challenge for you, so let's all stand up in a circle around this mat."

Within a few minutes, the boys are fully engaged in the Willow in the Wind exercise. They have been coached how to catch a leaning body with one of their legs canted back for support and with both hands extended out, palms forward, in front of them. Three boys, one at a time, stand in the middle of the circle, stiff as a board, with their arms folded across their chests and their eyes closed. They lean back and are "caught" and passed to others in the group, who also catch them and pass them along gently. The first boy to go is Enrique. Stephen chooses him to go first because, as he explains, "He was the first one to say something about being teased." The next boy, Isaiah, is a bit surprised when the boys, with the adult leaders' help, let him lean all the way back into an almost horizontal position and end up picking him up off the ground, raising him over their heads with their arms fully extended. With Isaiah suspended in the air, the leaders ask the boys to be quiet for a few moments, which they accomplish solemnly, and then to carefully bring Enrique all the way back down to the mat in safety.

Just before we break up on this fifth day, Howard asks those who did the exercise today to describe how it felt. Juan says, "I felt like I could really trust people." Isaiah says, "I felt like I was floating, I felt completely supported." Finally, Drake says that it felt like "there was nobody holding me up. And when I thought I was really falling, I said 'I can't do this,' but then they caught me again and I thought I could."

We end the group by responding to the boys' request to help decide who will be next in the Willow in the Wind activity when we meet next week. We then remind the boys to be respectful as they re-enter their classrooms for the remainder of the afternoon.

## Week 6: Making Lists

During these middle weeks of our group, our intention is to build on the supportive relationships that have formed in the group to tackle some difficult content. In this way, we are building on the basic ideas of attachment theory (Bowlby, 1988) in that we are providing the boys with a secure base from which they can take the risk of exploring new territory. Our intent has been to build a base of trust and safety in the group from which the boys can take the risk of discussing openly the challenges of growing up as a boy in our society.

Last week, we began this exploration by discussing what they get teased about as boys. This week we want to go deeper. We want to help them see that they get teased for acting in ways that are "outside the box" of social expectations for boys (e.g., for wearing pink, as in Stephen's story). We want them to be able to identify how they feel and what they do when they are teased and pressured to get "back in the box." We also want to begin to give them tools for fighting the pressures that exist for boys to conform to the limiting conventions of what it means to be a boy.

On this sixth meeting of our group, we begin with a story from Peter that is meant to describe a positive example of one of us acting "outside the box" in our own boyhood. We hope, in this way, to make it safe for the boys to begin to talk about and accept parts of themselves and their own experiences that do not easily conform to a standard definition of masculinity.

After the boys settle down, Peter says that he wants to tell a true story. He begins:

> When I was about 15 years old I had a paper route. Every day I would fold my papers, stuff them in my shoulder bags, and then ride around my neighborhood delivering them to all the houses on my route. One Friday afternoon, I was delivering my papers and thinking about a party I was going to have on Saturday night at my house. I had invited some of my friends and we were going to play ping-pong, play music, and eat lots of food.
>
> I was thinking about this party when I threw a paper into the driveway of Terry Walford's house. Terry was a girl in my class who was different than the rest of us. She kind of looked and walked funny and she didn't have any real friends at school at all. As I threw the paper, I saw her walking around the yard of her house by herself and I realized how lonely she must be. I decided that I would invite her to my party.
>
> Terry was really happy to be invited to the party and she was the first one to arrive the next night at my house. When my other friends showed up, one of them, Wally Jeffries, gave me a weird look when he saw Terry. Then he said, loud enough for everyone to hear, "Sick! What's *she* doing here?!" When I told him that I had invited her, I half expected him to leave the party. Maybe I just hoped that he would leave. But he ended up staying anyway and so did Terry. I remember feeling uncomfortable during the party about having invited Terry, but I also felt kind of proud, too.

After finishing his story, Peter gives this week's "talking pen" over to Howard who says:

> Peter's story is about getting teased for something, but doing it anyway because it was the right thing to do. Last week we made a list of the things you get teased for. Basically, it was a list about the things that people say a boy is not supposed to be—like being slow or bad at sports—and about the things that a boy is not supposed to do—like playing with girls or showing you care about school. This week, in contrast, we want you to tell us about the things that people say a boy is *supposed* to be and the things that people say a boy is *supposed* to do. What are those things? I'll write them down here on this big piece of paper.

In the 7 years that we have done this exercise with boys, it has been remarkable to us how consistent the items on this list are across different groups. In fact, for 6 out of 7 years, the first words on the list have been "tough" and "strong." What follows is the list that this year's group of fifth-grade boys came up with in reply to our question: "What is a boy supposed to be?"

> "Tough"
> "Strong"
> "Fast"
> "Not do girly things"
> "Don't do ballet"
> "Hang out with boys, not girls"
> "Do sports"
> "Not be a sissy"
> "Fearless"
> "Be big and bulky, like the Incredible Hulk"
> "Show no emotions"
> "Don't show anything"
> "Be happy or serious only"
> "No crybabies"
> "No tears"
> "Grunt"
> "Act cool"
> "Don't wear girly stuff"
> "Can't wear skirts or dresses"
> "Play with action figures, but not dolls"

Toward the end of this activity, Keith, one of the quieter but more astute boys in the group, shares the following story:

> If you're a boy, and somebody does something good for you, and you like it, you can't be all [he smiles brightly, with his eyes wide open]. You have to be more like [he narrows his eyes and tightens his mouth, nodding in a serious way]. You have to be cool.

Overall, the tone of the group while they are sharing these ideas and experiences is quiet and reflectively thoughtful. The boys seem to clearly understand the web of expectations and limitations that they are caught in. They also seem to be appreciative of the opportunity to put words to their experience, perhaps for the first time.

Still, we push on. Stephen next asks the boys to help make another list. He states: "If this list we just made is about what you are supposed to be, or not supposed to be as a boy, I want this next list to be about the names you get called when you do something different than these things. What are those names you get called?"

Not surprisingly, the following list of "names you get called" has also varied very little from year to year in our experience of running boys groups. Still, there is a certain impact when we capture the violence of these words as they are said and write them down in big letters on the butcher paper on the wall. The boys can hardly believe we are doing this exercise, from the look in their eyes. Our intention, of course, in acknowledging and writing these words down for all to see is not to further the power of these words, but to weaken the hold they have on boys. We mean this exercise to be a bit like pulling out splinters that have been lodged below the skin. The boys' list of names they get called includes:

"Gay"
"Fag"
"Midget"
"Dumb"
"Shorty"
"Girl"
"Bitch"
"Weakling"
"Short stuff"
"Retard"
"Stupid head"
"Sissy man"
"Girly men"

Astonishingly, the governor of California used that last phrase to publicly criticize his legislators during that particular week, and, obviously, the boys took note. They are excited at this point. They have nearly shouted out these epitaphs, slurs, and homophobic remarks, but not with anger and aggression. Instead, their words have been shouted with a sense of joyful release. In this conversation, the words themselves, not the boys, have finally become the target of critique.

Even though we are running short on time, we have one last question to ask the boys on this day. Howard says he would like their help making one final list. He is curious to know, he tells them, "what the effect is of being called these names. What happens to you when you get teased in this way, with these words?"

Once again, the boys are quick to respond. Their responses attest to both the violence that can happen internally as well as externally when boys are forced "into the box." These are their responses to Howard's questions:

"I want to close up and go away"
"I wanna quit"
"It's like the words get installed inside my head"
"I wanna cry"
"I want to close up and die"
"I sometimes get into fights over words"
"I think that maybe what they are saying is true"
"I call them names back"
"I beat them up"

As a way to get some closure on the depth of work that the group has done on this day, Peter chimes in after this last list has been created. "This is what I think," he says:

I think that this is what our group has been about. I think we have been creating a group, a place in this school, where you won't get called these names. You can come here and talk about things that you probably can't talk about in other places. We have made sure it has been a safe place. What we are going to try and figure out over the next few weeks is how you can be more of yourself both in this group and later when you are not in this group anymore. We don't want you to put yourself in a box or let others put you into a box. Today as a group we haven't been in the box. Today we have been breaking the box wide open.

At this point in the session, the boys are understandably growing somewhat antsy. We have covered a lot of ground and used a lot of words in the process. So we move to a physical activity. We end the group with three more boys, one at a time, standing in the middle of the circle of the rest of the boys and playing Willow in the Wind. The boys lean on one another, are caught, are lifted up over the group, and are brought safely down to the ground once again. They are learning to support one another.

## Week 7: Treasure Hunt

Because a number of the boys in our group also perform in a school chorus, attendance is low for our seventh meeting. It is a shame that only six boys are able to make it to the group today, but we notice the advantage of the smaller group right away. In general, the boys are more relaxed and a bit more forthcoming. From the very beginning of the session, even the quieter boys seem to be speaking more, and all of the boys seem to be listening better as well as being more responsive to one another's comments.

Howard starts off our seventh meeting with a personal story. Building on last week's topic, Howard says that he wants to tell the boys a story about a time when he acted "outside the box" and yet received support, not ridicule, from a friend for doing it:

> When I was 30, I went on a weeklong bike ride with some friends. We camped out along the way, had a lot of fun, and covered over 300 miles by the time we were finished. One night when we were sitting around the campfire, Tom, one of my friends, took out a bottle of tequila and passed it around saying, "No wimping out, everyone's gotta drink."
>
> I didn't feel like drinking, so I said that I didn't want any tequila when the bottle came my way. Tom brushed off my response as if it wasn't an option: "C'mon. Don't be a wimp!" He said, "You gotta drink like everyone else!" When Tom wasn't looking, I passed the bottle to the next person. A few minutes later, Tom asked me if I took a drink. Another friend of mine, Alan, jumped in and said, "Yeah, he did," even though he knew I had passed the bottle without sipping from it.
>
> I remember being shocked that here I was at 30 years old still facing pressure to take risks to prove that I was a man. But it also felt really good that my friend Alan had spoken up to support me. I think that this story is a good example of how we can help our friends refuse to be defined only by what is in the box.

After Howard finishes his story, Stephen reminds the boys about the exercise we had done last week in reference to "the boy box." He reminds them of the lists we had made: what they got teased for, what they thought they were supposed to be like as boys, what names they got called when they stepped outside that box, and, lastly, how they felt and responded when they were called those names. Stephen then says:

> Today we want to ask you to help us make another list. We want you to think of a part of yourself that is "outside the box." We think that all boys have many parts of themselves that don't fit with what you are "supposed to be" as a boy. We think that boys all feel pressure sometimes to cover up these parts of themselves in order to get back in the box and be like they think they are supposed to be. Like in Howard's story, he felt pressure for drinking even though he didn't want to drink. But he

also got support for being different, like you will here. So what are the parts of you that are "outside the box"?

Perhaps because of the work the boys have done over the past 6 weeks in terms of building trust and support in this group, Stephen's challenging prompt does not elicit silent resistance from the boys. Instead, they seem eager to talk about the parts of themselves that differ from the standard definition of what it means to be a boy. One by one, they make the following list:

> Curtis: "I like to keep my room organized."
> Isaiah: "I really like to hang out with girls."
> Drake: "I'd rather hang out with girls, too. Sometimes they are nicer."
> Paul: "This week, I've been having dreams at night about being pregnant. Also, I care about how I look and I'm in the Nutcracker ballet."
> Sorin: "I like to wear bright colors."
> Keith: "This probably sounds weird, but I like to clean the house."
> Enrique: "I'm really slow. I'm always being called a slowpoke."

In the conversational spaces between each boy describing what parts of himself are "outside the box" of conventional boyhood, there are also many supportive and empathetic comments made boy to boy: "I do a lot of the things Paul does," said Drake. "Yep! Me too," says Keith when he hears Curtis describe his passion for keeping his room organized. As a group leader, Stephen makes the boys aware of how in this exercise they have been supportive of each other regarding things that they may have been teased for out in the playground. He also tells them that the point of this exercise is to "help you find ways to support the parts of yourselves that you like but that you may hide because of teasing."

Drake follows this with the admission that he used to play with a friend named Sarah, but he stopped playing with her because he got teased about it too much. As a follow-up to what Drake says, Peter asks the boys how this group has been different for them compared with life "outside the group, in the playground or at school in general."

"Yeah, it's really different. I can share personal things," says Paul, who has perhaps shared the most "outside the box" aspects of himself of any of the boys, from being in ballet to dreaming of being pregnant. "I don't get this on the outside. It's easier to admit stuff in here because other people admit stuff, too," he continues.

Regarding his experience in the group, the normally quiet Enrique chimes in, "People understand me." Sorin adds his own thoughts:

> On the playground, if you can't climb something or jump three bars on the monkey bars, they think you're a wimp. If you can't be as good or better than the others, some boys will lie and say they are. It's not like that in here.

Stephen asks the boys to be aware of how they act on the playground this week and to see if they can find ways to be supportive of one another outside the group as well as inside the group. He then invites them to stand up and, since it is a lovely day outside, to walk quietly through the halls and meet down at the flagpole in the courtyard because "for our activity today, we are going to have a treasure hunt."

Once outside, one of the boys, Edward, is handed a small compass and asked to find north with the help of the others. Once they have gotten their bearings, the boys are then asked to find their way to the northwestern corner of the school where they will find their first clue hidden next to something orange. The boys run off down the sidewalk to find the northwest corner of the school and a clue that has been folded for them in the crease of an orange fire hydrant. After they find the clue, we ask the boys to agree on an order of who will open each of the clues. Keith is chosen to go first, and he opens the clue that reads: "Your first task is to stand in a circle from the tallest to the shortest. Your next task is for each of you to say something you appreciate about the shortest two boys in the group."

At first the boys are not very adept at offering appreciations. "He's really nice," they may say. As adult leaders, we coach them to make better contact with one another. We ask them to say the appreciation to the boy directly and to make it specific: "What makes Curtis nice? Say it to him directly. Look at him when you talk." After a while, the boys get the hang of it and are able to say things like, "I like that you are nice to me, Curtis, like when you came over to my house last weekend to play with me." By the time we have run half-way around the school pursuing and finding other clues, the boys are fully engaged in the activity and are able to think up increasingly complex appreciations. At one point toward the end of the treasure hunt, the ever-articulate Drake says to Theo, "Theo, you are really loving and kind, but it's kind of a secret." Theo smiles in response.

For a couple of the boys, the appreciations are mixed with heartfelt appraisals of certain weaknesses, such as when Curtis says to Sorin, "You are nice, but sometimes you are not." Interestingly, Sorin takes in this appraisal without getting defensive or mean, and we appreciate him for that ability to receive authentic feedback. We also make sure, however, that each boy is given multiple clear appreciations, if not from the boys, then from us. Sometimes, this is not an easy task, to remember something specific and positive about each boy on the spot. We find, however, that just speaking to the boy directly, noticing him in a kind and individual way in the group setting is enough. To the sometimes-difficult Keith, Stephen says, "I know that at first you didn't want to come to this group. I remember how you were on the first day. But now I see you show up every week and how you've been adding things to our discussion, and I appreciate you for making the decision to stay."

Over the years, our experience with this exercise has consistently been this: Instead of the fidgety, foot-shuffling discomfort you might expect boys to display doing such an exercise, what we have gotten is just the opposite. When it is their turn to appreciate another boy, their hands go up in eager willingness. When it is their turn to receive appreciations, they get quiet and sponge-like, seemingly absorbing the good words right into the pores of their calm, attentive faces. This absorption is best exemplified by Theo, who is often the quickest judge of what is "cool" (or not cool) in the group. As it turns out, on this day, he is last to receive appreciations. One might think a boy like Theo would be cynical about this exercise. One might imagine he would treat it dismissively, with a smirk and a turn of his head. Instead, when it is finally his turn after the group has run to the last corner of school, he gasps for breath as he tells us to wait because he isn't quite ready. He takes a moment to tie his shoe, then he stands up straight with an eager and open look on his face. He takes a deep breath and releases it before saying, "Okay, now I'm ready." When he does receive appreciations from each of the group members, he absorbs them with a big smile on his face.

An interesting side benefit of this appreciations exercise from our point of view as group leaders has been that we learn how different boys are seen and are appreciated from the perspective of their peers. We did not know, for example, that Sorin was seen by a few in the group as a good friend when he wanted to be, but that he could turn off that friendship at moment's notice. Nor did we know that Jesus was appreciated so widely for being so strong, when to us he appeared to be an average-sized boy.

One of our primary goals with this exercise, and with the group in general, has been to help create authentic contact among the boys. If a "boy in the box" withdraws not only from his own authentic self but also from real contact with others, we want to counteract that in this group. With this exercise, we work to accomplish this goal not only by helping the boys notice and hear from one another in positive ways, but also by helping the boys say things directly to one another, making eye contact in the process. For example, when Theo says "He's nice" about Sorin, we respond, "Look at Sorin, say, 'You're nice' and also tell us something that makes him nice." "You are generous to me," clarifies Theo.

As we finish with the appreciations exercise, standing in a tight-knit group on the sidewalk outside the front of the school, a spontaneous group hug emerges, initiated somehow by the boys. "All right, so this is where this is going," says Stephen as he reciprocates by putting his arms around the boys who have put their arms around him. This 7th week out of 10 with our boys has come to a close.

## Week 8: Trust Falling

As leaders, we have spent a lot of time thinking and talking about the role of experience in our boys group. Clearly, we have concepts that we want the boys to learn about—communication, conflict resolution, safety, trust, belonging—but we also want the boys to experience those concepts in and through the activities we plan for them each week. We believe that putting experience in the center of our group is a developmentally appropriate approach for working with all children. We know that children, and boys in particular, are working to make sense of the world through the use of their senses, their bodies, and their emotions, as well as their minds (Oaklander, 1978; Piaget, 1962). We know that we have to "scaffold" their learning of abstract concepts by giving them more concrete experiences to build on (Vygotsky, 1962). So last week when we wanted the boys to work on the concept of "direct communication," we did it through the experience of the treasure hunt where we encouraged them to give and receive appreciations directly to and from the other boys in the group.

This week, we want the boys to experience at a new level the trust and support that has been building in the group. We have been working over the past weeks to create an environment where it is safe to talk about things that boys don't often get support for expressing—feelings of vulnerability, for example. We have encouraged them to share parts of themselves that might in some way be "outside the box," and we have made sure that put-downs have not been accepted in our group sessions. Today, we hope that the boys walk away from the group knowing in their bones that they took a big risk but were able to count on the safety and support the group could provide for them. If boy culture in general is often fraught with having to prove how tough you are as an individual, at least for today we want the boys in our group to experience what it feels like to count on being a part of something larger than themselves.

"Okay, I'm glad to see you all back this week," says Peter as the boys settle in for our eighth meeting. He then continues:

This week is going to be a little bit different. Instead of starting off with a story, today we are going right into an activity that we have planned for you. Remember that these activities have been getting progressively more challenging each week because we want to see you guys show us how well you can work together as a group. In just a few weeks we will be going on our big adventure together—the one we have been building up to for weeks—a Friday night hike up Mt. Nicolas. But before we go on that adventure, we need to see you work together well in school so that we know we can count on you when you get outside of school.

Okay, I want you to think of a burning building for a minute. The building is tall, and there are fires on the lower floors of the building, so there are firefighters there with those large, round trampoline things to catch people as they jump from the building. The toughest thing is for those people in the building to be able to trust that the firefighters will be there to catch them when they jump. We want each of you in this group to be able to count on each other in the same way. Today we are going to do a trust fall. It goes like this. . . .

Peter finishes explaining the activity to the boys who are now excitedly finishing their lunches. Before long, we have two thick safety mats in place and the boys have chosen the order in which they will fall—and be caught—by the rest of the boys. We teach the boys how to hold their arms bent slightly at the elbow with their palms face up. We remind them to bend their knees and put one foot slightly behind them for more support (they learned this stance originally in the Willow in the Wind activity). When they are lined up in two parallel rows and their arms are out, Howard leans into their hands and they catch him, demonstrating the group's ability to catch even an adult. We decide that the boys are taking the activity seriously enough to allow the first boy, Drake, to climb up onto the window ledge. Once he gets up there, about 3 feet off the ground, he looks back nervously over his shoulder. Peter and Howard are standing closest to the window ledge, both with a hand supporting Drake's back as he teeters on the 6-inch ledge. Stephen is positioned at the opposite end of the column of boys, ready to give extra support in gently catching Drake's head when he falls.

For a moment, both Keith and Sorin are off task. They are standing across from each other with their arms out like everyone else, yet they are joking around and talking to each other, not paying attention to Drake at all. Seeing this, Drake makes a worried sound and asks for Peter's help to climb down off the ledge. "If you don't want to go today, or at all, that's totally fine, Drake," says Peter. "But I want to ask you," he continues, "if you needed to say something to anyone in the group that would make you feel more supported, that would make you feel like you could do this challenge, what would you say and who would you say it to?"

"Some of them were goofing around and I didn't feel like they were gonna catch me," Drake says.

"Okay," says Stephen, "what could you say to them directly about what you need?"

"Sorin and Keith, I want you guys to stop goofing around and talking and to tell me that you'll catch me," Drake says directly to them both. Surprisingly, using a serious tone with no hint of defensiveness, Sorin replies, "Okay, we are going to catch you, Drake." Keith nods.

Drake then scrambles up onto the ledge again. He peers over his shoulder, still looking nervous, but this time he is greeted by all 10 boys looking up at him silently with their arms outstretched. "Ready to fall," Drake says as he crosses his arms over his chest and looks away from the boys once again. "Fall away," respond the boys in unison. Like a flat board, Drake begins to fall away from the window ledge and seconds later he is resting in the arms of the boys. Peter encourages the group to hold Drake for three seconds without saying anything—he counts off slowly "1 . . . 2 . . . 3 . . . "—and then he tells them that they can gently put Drake down on the mat, which they do.

Now there is real excitement in the room as the next boys in line begin to clamor for their turn. Drake says, "That was cool!" and joins the line of catchers. Theo climbs up on the window ledge and the game of trust, a game with real consequences and real effects, begins again.

During this eighth session of our group, there are two boys, Enrique and Keith, who decline to do the trust fall. When they do, Stephen says:

> As I said before, it is totally fine if you don't want to do this exercise. In fact, it's great that you were both willing to say that you don't want to go. Like in Howard's story about his bike trip, it's important to be able to say when you don't want to do something. It's important to be able to say no sometimes even when you are feeling pressure because everyone else is doing it. Good for you, Enrique and Keith!

When all of the boys who wanted to do the trust fall have had a chance to fall back and be caught, Howard settles the boys down in a circle on the mat. He asks the boys what they experienced doing the trust fall. Curtis says that he was "kinda afraid no one would catch me. Then I thought in my head that I could trust these guys, and they did catch me." A number of other boys talk excitedly about both the risk they took and the support they received. Finally, Howard says, "I gotta tell you guys, I have this thing that when I get up into heights, I'm scared. And when I watched you go up on that ledge, I got sweaty palms."

"You were scared?" says James with a bit of attitude, "See, I like heights." Howard responds: "James, I feel like you're telling me that what I felt was not okay." James looks at Howard and says, "Oh, sorry. I'm just not afraid of heights. I am afraid of bees, though." In reply, Howard says, "Okay, let's do this. Before we go today, let's each say one thing that scares us."

The boys come up with a list of fearful things that includes more bees (Edward); getting another operation (Drake); heights (Curtis); and, from Theo, usually the most stoic one in the group, the following thoughtful response: "I think ahead a lot and worry about random things. Like I can't trust people's knots on a hammock, or I worry about a bridge falling when I'm crossing it." A number of other boys make quiet sounds of recognition as Theo speaks and no one criticizes anyone else for the fears the boys have admitted to. Howard thanks the boys for not only being brave enough to do the trust fall, but also for admitting one thing they are afraid of. Week 8 comes to a close.

# Week 9: Talking Cards

Too fast, it seems, we have come to the last couple of weeks with our boys. In planning this ninth week, we as leaders discuss how this group could easily continue all year long. We talk about how we could spend so much more time and attention on the topics and experiences we have briefly covered over the past 8 weeks: trust, risk, vulnerability, strength, belonging, contact. Part of the reason we limit the group to 10 weeks, though, is so that we can recruit another group of boys for another 10-week session before the school year is out. Still, it is not easy to begin closing out our time with this particular group of boys.

We face a big issue in ending this group: We have been successful in helping boys make better contact with themselves and one another in the group; now we need to think about how to make sure these benefits don't end as the group closes. To address this issue, we have planned the activities for the final 2 weeks of the group to address dual objectives: (1) We will be closing our experience together as a group by revisiting what we have learned, and (2) we will be helping the boys think about how they can find BAM!-like supports outside the group once our time together has ended.

Stephen begins the ninth week of our group by reminding the boys that we will be meeting only two more times. "This will be our last time meeting together at school. But next week," he says, "we will be going on our Mt. Nicolas adventure on Friday night. So who remembered to bring in their permission slips?"

We have been talking about our Mt. Nicolas adventure for weeks with the boys. We have planned an evening outing that includes a nighttime walk with flashlights up a wooded trail that will culminate, at the end of the dark trail, with warm dessert being shared with dads and other supportive males from the boys' lives. In past years, we have planned different activities. One year it was a Saturday canoe trip across the river to an island for a picnic and a series of group challenges (e.g., hacking down invasive weeds with sticks, a treasure hunt that included looking for and cleaning up trash, etc.). This will be the first year, however, that we made it a priority to include supportive men from the boys' home lives as a way of extending the benefits of our work together in the group. There is more on this final adventure in next week's section of this narrative account.

On this ninth week, we are alone with the boys finding a way to close up our experience together. As a way to begin this closing, Peter asks the boys to think back on our 8 weeks together and all the things we have done. "Let's try and remember all the things we have done in the same order we did them," he says. Over the next few minutes, the boys call out and describe things that have happened in the group, often correcting each other as to what happened when. "We did the haunted house!" says Edward. "No, first we had to get everyone over the electric fence so we could go to Burgerville!" says Sorin.

Not surprisingly, the activities that stand out most in the boys' minds are the ones involving physical challenge. They don't, for example, mention the stories that we as leaders have told them. But once the activities of the group over the past 8 weeks have been reconstructed by the boys, Peter asks them another question: "So these are all the things we have done together as a group. But why did we do all these things?" Almost immediately, answers to this question are offered by the boys: "Trust," says one. "Teamwork," says another. And Keith, a boy who came into the group as a kind of social outcast, says, "To make friends."

Peter then tells the boys he has an activity he would like them to do. He takes out a small, old-fashioned suitcase with brass corners and dramatically opens it to show hundreds of Talking Cards inside. The Talking Cards (Mortola, 2003) are made of random images from magazines, calendars, and children's books that have been laminated on $6 \times 8$-inch pieces of construction paper to give them some heft, durability, and glossiness. Peter takes the cards out of the box and spreads them on the floor. There are images of waterfalls, sailing boats, families at Thanksgiving dinner, dogs wearing life jackets in a canoe, and many more. With all these colorful pictures spread out on the floor, Peter now has the boys' attention. He describes the activity he wants them to do:

I want you to look through all these pictures on the floor until you find three cards that you like. The first card I want you to pick should represent something about you before you came into this group. The second card should represent something about your experience here in the group over the past 8 weeks. The third card I want you to pick should be about something you want to have happen in the future.

We have done this closing activity in the past with our boys groups and it has always been successful. Still, there is a moment or two as the boys are noisily sorting through all the images when we wonder what will come of it. Will they just pick images that are silly? Will they not "get" the activity at all? Worse yet, will they decide it would be cooler to be cynical about the cards they pick or the things that they have to say about them? We take a leap of faith with this activity, but it is a leap based on past successes. The random and large set of images we have collected seems to allow each of the boys to find something that speaks to his own experience. Paradoxically, the boys are able to express very personal and meaningful reflections about their own experience in the group by talking about and through the random and impersonal images they find on these cards. To us, the success of this exercise is an example of how indirect communication with boys can actually allow more direct contact with them.

We let the boys take a long 5 minutes to root through all the cards and have fun doing it. Peter then calls the boys to order and tells them: "We are very interested in what you have to say about your cards: about who you were before the group, what your experience in the group has been, and what you hope for in the future." Although each of the boys eventually takes a turn talking about his cards, we have selected three responses representative of the group comments on this day, transcribed as follows. At the beginning of this exercise, Peter picked a toy shark that lives in the counseling office as today's "talking object." Below, Peter references this "talking shark" in starting out the activity with the Talking Cards.

*Isaiah*

| | |
|---|---|
| *Peter:* | All right, we need the talking shark. Curtis, since you have it do you want to start? |
| *Curtis:* | No. |
| *Peter:* | Okay, would anybody like to start? Isaiah has his hand up. . . |
| *Isaiah:* | Yesss. |
| *Peter:* | It's all yours. You tell us about all three of your cards, one at a time. |
| *Isaiah:* | Okay. The first one is really cute. It's a walrus [laughter] . . . and you see it's covering its eye. Its eye with its hand . . . and that's because before I came into this group, I used to be like shy about meeting new people. And so that's what that resembles . . . |
| *Peter:* | That's cool, Isaiah. |
| *Isaiah:* | And then this one resembles what we did in the group . . . |
| *Peter:* | Make sure everyone can see the picture . . . [Isaiah holds up his picture of a group of people helping each other climb up ledges in the middle of a waterfall]. . . . So, there are people walking on a waterfall . . . |
| *Isaiah:* | It looks like they're working together to help one person up. Or they're working together to help each other. And that's what we did in this group. |
| *Peter:* | That's what you experienced in the group . . . |
| *Isaiah:* | And the last one . . . was really cool . . . |
| *Peter:* | Make sure everybody sees it . . . |
| *Theo:* | Frozen blueberries . . . |
| *Sorin:* | [gently teasing him] You wanna be a frozen blueberry? |
| *Isaiah:* | Close, but no . . . |
| *Peter:* | His turn to talk, guys. I want him to talk . . . |
| *Isaiah:* | Okay, and, like, and it would symbolize us being close as friends . . . |
| *Peter:* | Nice . . . |
| *Isaiah:* | And then I don't know what the ice would symbolize . . . |
| *Peter:* | Cold friends . . . |
| *Isaiah:* | Yeah. |
| *Howard:* | That's cool . . . |
| *Peter:* | Cool friends! |
| *Theo:* | Cool, exactly! [laughter] |
| *Isaiah:* | Okay. |
| *Sorin:* | Thank you. [receives the talking shark from Isaiah] |

*Sorin*

| | |
|---|---|
| *Peter:* | All right. Sorin has to go next. Sorin, my man . . . |

| | |
|---|---|
| *Sorin:* | My first one that I picked for my first one, um, I felt kind of alone . . . I have this one, this little tree thing in the desert [holding up a picture of a single plant surrounded by sand] . . . |
| *Peter:* | The Yucca plant in the desert . . . |
| *Sorin:* | Yeah. And then this is my other one. My other one . . . |
| *Peter:* | [interrupting some chatter] You guys looking at these cards? |
| *Sorin:* | [holding up a picture of sea plants clinging to a rock being washed over by waves] I'm one of the little, one palm-tree thingee. |
| *Peter:* | Yeah. |
| *Sorin:* | And all the waves are like . . . doinggg . . . |
| *Peter:* | So what is this about you? |
| *Sorin:* | It's just kind of, I used to be kind of alone. Just like the other . . . that, that one . . . |
| *Peter:* | The Yucca plant, yeah, they're kind of similar . . . I'm excited to hear your next one here . . . |
| *Sorin:* | [holding up a card with a colorful image of an abstract painting] And um, when I was in the group I kinda felt, um, colorful . . . |
| *Theo:* | [thoughtfully] Colorful . . . |
| *Sorin:* | Yeah . . . it's all kinds of colorful . . . |
| *Theo:* | That's tight . . . |
| *Peter:* | [to Sorin] What does that mean? . . . |
| *Sorin:* | Um, I just felt like, or it could be just, I felt like more comfortable with being with other people, like see I was one little color with others . . . |
| *Peter:* | You know what I think is so interesting is that you, more than one time in the group, you brought up how you like to wear different colors . . . and how boys get teased for wearing different colors . . . |
| *Sorin:* | Oh yeah! And that. |
| *Peter:* | I think that's really cool. |
| *Drake:* | He's wearing different colors right now . . . |
| *Peter:* | Yeah, your green hat and your blue shirt. . . . What's your last card? |
| *Sorin:* | Um, and it's new, I'm gonna share this one [holds up a picture of a boy in a swimming pool sitting in a pink, inflatable hot rod] It's, um, it's . . . I want to have that in the future. And it would really just be fun and I like pink and um . . . yeah, and I want that car, I want that car . . . |
| *Peter:* | It's a pink, inflatable hotrod. |
| *Sorin:* | I want that in the pool and I want a real car like that. |
| *Peter:* | I want the sun that shines in the picture . . . |
| *Sorin:* | Yeah, and, I also have a flamingo necklace . . . |
| *Peter:* | Oh look at that! A flamingo necklace that's pink and yellow, colorful . . . |

Theo:       Oh, that thing is so tight ...

**Jesus**

Jesus:      In the beginning ...
Peter:      In the beginning ...
Jesus:      I was all freaky ... [shows his first picture of a dark cave and a glowing light] ...
Peter:      It was all freaky ... a cave with light and darkness in it ...
Jesus:      That's why it's all freaky ...
Peter:      Were you like that or was the group like that?
Jesus:      I was ...
Peter:      You were a little bit like that? [Jesus nods] What's freaky mean?
Jesus:      I don't know ...
Jorge:      Scared ...
Jesus:      No, it mean's like weird ...
Peter:      A little weird. You felt weird or you think other people thought you were weird?
Jesus:      Other people thought I was weird.
Peter:      Uh, huh.
Jesus:      And then I came to the group ... [shows second picture of a crew working together on a keeled-over sailboat] ...
Theo:       Teamwork ...
Peter:      People sailing on a boat together ...
Jesus:      Yeah, and it looks like the boat's, like, going to go one way ...
Peter:      Yeah, it does. ... So was that different? If the other card was about feeling freaky, this is about feeling ...
Theo:       It's like he said, teamwork ...
Jesus:      Teamwork ...
Peter:      So you're connected, you're not alone maybe. I'm saying that, but that's my experience in the past years, is that boys feel less alone when they come to these groups ...
Jesus:      Yeah ... and I wanna be [showing his third picture of a tall Saquaro cactus] freaky still ... [laughter] ...
Stephen:    And you wanna be what?
Jesus:      Freaky ...
Stephen:    Freaky?
Peter:      A cactus with thorns ...
Theo:       Like those bumper stickers that say "Keep Portland Weird" ...
Peter:      Yeah, I like that bumper sticker, too ... "Keep Portland Weird" ... that's a good bumper sticker. ... Yeah I hope you guys keep freaky too because that's what we don't. ... We see boys at ten years old start to lose their freakiness and you have to become like macho man, no feelings, no nothing ... and we don't want you to become that ...

*Paul:*     [sings] I want to be, a macho man . . .

*Peter:*    Yeah, it's better to sing and dance it than it is to actually be it . . .

Over the past few years of running these BAM! groups, we have observed a theme consistently emerge on this closing day: the loneliness of boys. Many boys have described how they had felt alone or lonely before the group started and that somehow their experience in the group has helped them to feel less alone. We could not have asked for a better outcome to be expressed by our group participants. We know that many of the troubling issues boys will face as they move into adolescence have to do with getting "cut off" and isolated from their own emotional experience as well as from contact with others (e.g., disengagement from school, harm to self and others, emotional shutdown, etc.).

Jesus gives a good example of getting "cut off" from both himself and others in the transcribed passage above: At the outset of the group he imagined other boys thought he was "freaky" or "weird." At the end of the group, however, he asserts two things: that the group has helped him experience more of a sense of "togetherness" or "teamwork," but he also makes it clear that he wants to maintain his uniqueness—his "freakiness"—and we move to support him in that as well.

We are gratified to know that so many boys over the years have had an experience of rich and supportive contact in the BAM! groups. In this way, we see BAM! groups serving as an antidote for the loneliness and alienation that boys too frequently experience. In our final meeting with the boys next week, we work to extend their experience of supportive contact by including significant adult men from the boys' lives in our final BAM! group experience.

# Week 10: Found in the Woods

It is raining on the night of our last big adventure—our outdoor adventure. Still, most of the boys show up equipped with a raincoat or at least a fleece jacket. The boys' dads, uncles, neighbors, and recruited mentors—over half of the boys in the group had no father involved in their lives—have dropped the boys off at the bottom of Mt. Nicolas at 7 p.m. on a dusky, wet, January evening. These supportive adult men in the boys' lives have then driven up to the top of the 1,000-foot wooded mountain near downtown. Our plan is for the boys to walk up to meet the men at a covered picnic area near the top, but, of course, we have some ideas about how to make the walk a bit more interesting.

For years, we have been using the "reward" of a big closing adventure for our group as a way to reinforce for the boys the importance of them working well together in the group during our weekly sessions. By anticipating this closing adventure, we have been able to emphasize on a week-to-week basis that we needed to see the boys demonstrate skills in working together and being supportive of one another in order for us to be able to trust them enough to take them on an adventure where the risks are even greater. To this end, supporting one another physically (getting over the electric fence, catching one another in the trust fall, etc.) as well as emotionally (giving empathetic responses when one member talks about his alcoholic mother, avoiding put-downs, etc.) was stressed as the ways healthy groups work together to achieve goals. In short, working toward the final adventure has served as motivation for the boys also to move toward demonstrating the goals we as leaders have had for the group.

When all the boys have gathered at the bottom of Mt. Nicolas on this rainy evening, we call for their attention—they have been having fun just running around playing tag—to tell them one more story. Peter tells the boys that there is warm cocoa and cake waiting for them at the top of the mountain where the adults are, but that we have one last challenge as a group before we can get there. He tells them with a straight face that a fierce ogre lives on this mountain and that it only comes out at night, when it's raining. He tells them, as they smirk and laugh nervously in playful disbelief, that this fierce ogre will take any boy as victim who is isolated from the group, so it is very important that the boys stay together.

As we begin the 1-mile-long hike up the mountain, the ogre makes his presence known in various ways. When one of our boys steps in an ogre track, for example, he loses the use of his leg and has to be carried for a time by the rest of the group before he can regain use of his leg. Four boys are told that they had caught a brief glimpse of the ogre's shadow, and, therefore, they each lose the use of their eyes for a time. These boys are then blindfolded and have to be led arm in arm up the trail by the remaining group members who can see. Occasionally, the ogre (Stephen) jumps out from behind a tree and makes horrific growling and gnashing sounds before it disappears again. At one point, a blindfolded Keith gets cut off from the group and starts staggering around briefly on his own. It is Isaiah who finds Keith and kindly makes sure he gets reconnected with the group before the ogre gets him.

Moving up the mountain, we arrive at a public water faucet after the boys have just finished the difficult work of carrying each other up a steep part of the trail. The boys dash to the water faucet and gulp down the cold water. In the sheer exhilaration of the moment, James emphatically states: "This is the best water I have ever tasted!"

Just as we are about to make it to the top of the trail and our rendezvous with the supportive men who are awaiting our arrival, Curtis arrives late and comes running down the hill to join the group for the last few hundred yards. The boys immediately make up a story about Curtis having been lost in the woods, and they proceed to carry him all the way up to the shelter where the adults and dessert wait. Because campfires are not allowed on Mt. Nicolas, two volunteers (both of whom had led boys groups in past years) have improvised by lighting a number of candles and placing them in a circle on the cement floor of the shelter. As the boys rush into the shelter, the adult men who had brought them give them each a big hug and welcome them. Having been coached by volunteer leaders in advance, the men help a wonderful thing to happen next.

Drawn to playing with the candles, all the boys cluster around the flames in a relaxed, sprawling, and somewhat mesmerized group on the floor. The men spontaneously stand in a circle around the boys and are formally thanked by Stephen for taking the time to come to this important event. Peter then asks the men to each think of one good quality that they appreciate about the boy they have accompanied and that they would hate to see lost as the boy grows older. One man named Paul starts by telling the rest of the group that he is Curtis's neighbor and friend. He then speaks directly to Curtis, saying:

> Curtis, I know you are going to be a good man because of the gentle way that you play with my daughter, Sylvia. I especially appreciate the way you played with her during that time when she was getting picked on by other kids in the neighborhood. I always trust you with her and hope you never lose that kindness.

Next, Theo's mentor says to him: "I really like the way you are with your friends, Theo, how you put your arm around them and make them laugh. I hope you never lose your ability to be warm with your friends." Another mentor appreciates Edward by saying, "I really like the way you take school seriously, Edward. You love to learn and I hope you hold onto that when you get into middle school."

James's father is next. James looks up at his father's glowing face as his father says:

> James, I love your creativity. You are always making something or working on some project. It is so fun to see you get so engaged and focused. I know that sometimes it's harder for you to focus like that in school, but I hope you always keep that creativity.

When it is Peter's turn, he tells the group that he is about to have his own first child, a boy, and that he hopes his son will have the best qualities of each of the boys. Peter states:

> I hope my son has Theo's leadership, Sorin's ability to wear bright colors, Paul's love of dance, Curtis's kindness, Jesus's ability to make friends, Enrique's strength, Edward's sense of humor, James's ability to speak his mind, and Isaiah's emotional honesty.

While the men are giving their appreciations, some of the boys look up at them as they speak, others sit quietly playing with the candle wax, all of them listen intently. As the "campfire moment" comes to a close, Howard asks the boys to make sure and tell the men in their lives more about what we have done in the BAM! group over these last 10 weeks. He also thanks the men who have come for all the support they are giving the boys as they transition into middle school.

You can always tell it's a successful party when the guests don't want to leave. Over cake and cocoa, conversation among the men flows as the boys play games and run in the shadows of the big trees around the picnic area. The rain is still lightly falling—but there is shelter—as our boys group comes to a close.

# BAM! Instructions

## Overview

In BAM! Instructions we will address the practicalities of beginning a BAM! group, consider some of the finer points of BAM! group facilitation, and outline detailed instructions to allow you to replicate each of the BAM! group sessions.

## Initiating a BAM! Group

### Collecting Data and Proposing a BAM! Group

To begin crafting a BAM! group proposal, start with a clear description of some of the challenges that boys face in your community. Before promoting the group to others, gather data on how the boys in your area are doing. A good place to begin is to gather data from schools and local youth-serving agencies. Many schools now make it easy to find data that are disaggregated by gender. The initial section of the guidebook also outlines some of the data regarding boys' strengths as well as challenges.

Next, consider how your community will respond to a BAM! group. Some regions are more invested in traditional models of masculinity and may be less receptive to BAM! groups. For example, at a recent BAM! workshop in a rural setting, a participant said, "Boys need to be tough and stoic. I was out with my boy over the weekend branding cows. If he was to get all weepy and sad for the cows we couldn't have done our job." Clearly, certain tasks like branding cows require stoicism, but other parts of a boy's life are not well served by such disengagement. We shared data illustrating the negative impact of boys' disengagement and talked about the ways BAM! groups can help them be more connected.

Knowing the data and having considered your community's receptivity to BAM!, you are ready to prepare an initial proposal. Consider the factors that make BAM! groups unique, such as the following descriptors from the various proposals we have put together over the years:

- A chance for boys to experience a sense of belonging to school
- An opportunity for boys to consider what it means to be a healthy man
- A new type of social experience where boys can work together without put-downs
- An opportunity for boys to practice being relationally skilled

You can see how each of these descriptions emphasizes a different facet of BAM! groups that may play differently in different communities.

When you present your plan, share the potential benefits of offering BAM! groups. We have begun collecting data that show that participation in BAM! groups helps boys feel more connected to their schools, have more awareness of the social pressures they face, and experience safety—not shame—in a group setting.

## Responding to Parental Concerns

You will need formal permission from parents in order to have their sons participate in a BAM! group (see Sample Permission Form in the Appendix). Parental response to BAM! groups has been overwhelmingly positive. When parents have voiced reservations, their concerns have fallen into three categories: (1) apprehension about the risk of the physical activities; (2) fear that the goal of the group is to turn their boys into girls; and (3) belief that BAM! group participation identifies their son as troubled. We suggest possible ways of addressing such concerns in the paragraphs that follow.

**Physical Risks**   The types of activities described in this book are commonly performed in camps and other youth settings. Activities such as these, by their very nature, are highly physical, active, and participatory. Thoughtful attention when performing these challenges leads to an environment where they can be done safely. You can respond to concerns about safety by describing the precautions outlined in the instructions for each activity. In addition to allaying parental concerns, you will want to check with the school or organization hosting the group to discuss issues of liability.

**Turning Boys Into Girls**   Another concern that you may hear from parents is that these groups are trying to turn their boys into girls. In response, we describe how BAM! groups are really about helping boys stay true to their own experiences, feelings, and interests while also learning new communicative and relational skills. BAM! group participation is not about being a boy *or* being emotionally competent; it is about being both.

**Is My Son in Trouble?**   BAM! groups are different from many groups commonly offered for boys in that they focus on promoting positive relationships as opposed to extinguishing negative behaviors. Historically, most groups serving boys have focused on reducing behavioral issues such as anger or impulsivity. Given how boys have been served, it is possible that parents will assume that this is a group for problem behavior. This misunderstanding may make parents defensive. Emphasize the positive goals of BAM! groups when responding to this concern.

## Getting Appropriate Referrals

BAM! groups can be offered within schools, churches, after-school programs, scouting organizations, leadership courses, athletic programs, camps, or any other places where boys gather. The stories from this book describe a group of fifth-grade boys in a school district where students transition to middle school in sixth grade. Our boys were between 9 and 12 years old. We chose this age group because fifth graders are very aware of the social influences on them but still generally maintain some openness. Also, we know that, as they move to middle school they will face increasing pressure to disengage and repress parts of themselves. The activities described in the BAM! Instructions section can be modified for other ages, but the philosophy of the facilitators should remain consistent.

BAM! groups are strengths-based groups. They are not intended to directly or completely reduce behavioral and emotional problems. Referral sources may incorrectly assume that this is a group for boys with discipline problems. This misunderstanding may lead to inappropriate referrals. We want to be realistic about the potential of BAM! groups and clear about the boys we can serve best.

It is important to note that higher-risk boys tend to adhere to more traditional forms of masculinity. Boys who bully, for example, will likely cling to traditional models of males as aggressor and may feel threatened by a BAM! group, leading to more defensive and challenging behavior. It will be more difficult to effectively deliver the message of BAM! groups to a homogenous collection of high-risk or "gender conservative" boys.

It is important to have the group represent a range of boys and a range of masculinities. The group described in this book was made up of boys who at times were bullies and others who were at times victims. We had a range of cultural and racial backgrounds. We had students who were athletic and students who were artistic. The broader the range of boys, the richer the discussion and the greater the opportunity for group members to explore different ideas of what it means to be a boy.

The ideal number of boys in a BAM! group is between six and ten. Any larger and the group will likely be more didactic, limit students' opportunities to share, and create more behavioral issues. Any smaller and the group may not allow for dynamics between and among boys that create learning opportunities. It is best to keep BAM! groups closed. In other words, once the group gets started, don't bring in new group members. After the second session, have all the boys commit to doing their best to make it to the remainder of the sessions.

## Recruiting Boys

We think it is important to advertise BAM! groups so that boys see them as cool. We suggest using language that speaks to boys. We don't, for example, describe BAM! groups as focused on learning more about feelings. For boys, it is a group in which they get to do fun activities, face physical challenges, have adventures, hang out, and be a part of something exciting.

Over time, the group may become part of the school culture and recruiting may become easier. At Meadow Elementary School, we have been leading BAM! groups for 7 years. Stories about the big adventures that past groups have taken have become lore among the incoming classes of students. In the boys' minds, the group has become something of a rite for all boys at the school.

In this section, we have addressed some of the larger issues of initiating a BAM! group in your setting. In the next section, we address some of the particular issues involved in facilitating a BAM! group.

# Facilitating a BAM! Group

The positive impact of BAM! groups often arises out of the leaders' skillful work. In this section we examine the characteristics of a BAM! leader, explore the art of leading a BAM! group, and reflect on some of the dynamic tensions group leaders must balance. We also discuss how to manage group members' behavior, and conclude the chapter with an excursion into the unique challenges and opportunities for female and male leaders.

## Qualities of BAM! Group Leaders

We know that children learn from what is modeled for them (Bandura, 1986), and that the boys in our groups not only watch who we are as individuals but how we interact with group members and other adults. With this in mind, BAM! leaders must carefully model respect, emotional fluency, and the appropriate regulation of those emotions—all skills we want the boys to learn. We are keenly aware that we teach them just as much about healthy relationships with what we show them as we do with what we tell them.

Group leaders must also be mindful of their assumptions about boys. To truly support group members, group leaders must examine their own history with boys and men. Are there ways in which your social history may interfere with your own ability to lead BAM! groups? Do you have a history of abuse that affects your perceptions of males? How comfortable are you around boys' physicality and silly behavior? Do groups of boys intimidate you? These are questions which a BAM! leader must address before the group even starts. We believe that successful leaders of BAM! groups are able to:

- Connect with boys
- Look beyond boys' bravado, knowing that boys sincerely want to be real with each other
- Understand and have compassion for the dilemmas boys face
- Invite boys into activities rather than impel them
- Provide a spark of enthusiasm into the activities

As intentional as we are in running BAM! groups, so much of what happens in the group cannot be planned. Situations arise requiring leaders to think on their feet and make decisions about the direction of the group several times each session. For this reason, we think creativity, flexibility, and a highly developed sense of fun are key attributes for a BAM! group leader to possess. (For more on group leadership skills, see Kottler, 2001, and Oaklander, 1978).

## The Art of BAM! Group Facilitation

Ideally, co-facilitators lead BAM! groups. However, we understand that this is a luxury that many organizations are not able to provide. If you are offering the group by yourself, you might want to limit the size of the group and adjust some of the activities out of concern for safety. It might also be worthwhile to consult with a colleague or supervisor to help sort out issues regarding group dynamics among the boys and your personal reactions to what happens each week in the group. Whether you have a co-leader or not, allow time to reflect on the dynamics and progress of the group after each session and to create a plan for the session to come. We have found that this debriefing time is the most important source of ideas for where the group needs to go next.

As BAM! group leaders, we demonstrate our value for strong relational skills by how we respond to the boys. We acknowledge boys for demonstrating qualities such as thoughtfulness, vulnerability, and openness. We give them credit when they demonstrate caring for others, exercise impulse control, or stick with things that are hard. We also acknowledge when a boy acts outside the limiting social norm. For example, we might say, "That is cool, James, how you take care of your little sister. So often, boys feel like they have to pick on their little brothers and sisters."

Understanding the importance of contact, we try not to mediate interactions between boys but encourage them to speak directly to each other. For example, if a boy says, "I didn't like the way *he* was goofing off during the activity," we would ask the boy to speak directly to the second boy saying something like, "I didn't like the way *you* were goofing off during the activity." This redirection helps the boys connect with each other and develops their ability to communicate directly and assertively.

## Keeping Balanced as a BAM! Leader

As BAM! leaders, we have come to realize that successful group leadership is really based on the ability of group leaders to hold a creative tension between sometimes contradictory goals. Here are three sets of these polarities that we work hard to keep in balance:

**Balancing Planned Activities With Spontaneity**    The typical BAM group session contains these elements:

- The facilitator tells a story that quiets the boys and entices them into the session.
- Participants share their personal reactions to the story.
- The group does a physical activity that enlivens the message of the story.
- The group closes with a summary that helps reinforce learning and shore up vulnerabilities before the boys leave.

More often than not, however, our well-laid plans change based on surprises that occur and opportunities that present themselves. There are teachable moments in a group that present themselves more elegantly than we could ever have planned. Often these moments arise out of a group member's comments or reactions to an activity. Being clear about our objectives and monitoring the boys' reactions help us to know when to veer from our original plan.

One day, for example, we were talking about the pressures boys face. That particular day, fewer boys were in attendance, and those who were there were very engaged in a conversation in reaction to the opening story. We decided to extend the conversation and forego the physical challenge that day. The boys appeared comfortable as they took their time and participated in a discussion with a good bit of natural give and take. It made sense on that day to follow their lead.

**Balancing Support With Risk** The boys in BAM! groups are able to move more deeply into honest and open participation in the group the more we supportively lower the threats that may impede such participation. We use Bowlby's (1988) description of attachment theory as a touchstone: "All of us, from cradle to grave, are happiest when life is organized as a series of excursions, long or short, from a secure base." Our work with boys in BAM! groups provides a secure base from which they can take physical, emotional, and cognitive excursions that support their growth and move them toward realizing the goals of the group.

We provide both physical comforts (e.g., snacks, beanbag chairs, and a casual atmosphere) and physical challenges to the boys. We provide emotional supports (e.g., setting clear group ground rules and modeling our own openness) while at the same time challenging the boys to take the risk of talking about their own feelings and to empathize with others. We also provide intellectual supports—such as helping the boys see that they can have a broader repertoire of behavior and experience—as we challenge them to examine the ideas behind traditional male socialization. In these ways, our work in BAM! groups moves back and forth between the poles of providing both supports and challenges at the physical, emotional, and cognitive levels of the boys' experience.

**Balancing Safety With Fun** BAM! groups are supposed to be fun. At the same time, safety is our primary concern when encouraging the boys to take emotional risks and engage in physically risky activities. Although it may sound contradictory, we as leaders are *fierce* in our adherence to creating a safe and fun environment for the boys. We do not tolerate emotionally hurtful put-downs. We also do not tolerate goofing around during the risky activities. Our fierceness is not about controlling the boys, it is about providing enough support for them to take the risk of experiencing something new.

Our own experience is a good barometer of where we stand on the safety and fun continuum. We might notice our voices getting louder, or we might notice ourselves feeling angry, or we may hear ourselves repeating pleas for cooperation too many times. Some boys may be uncomfortable with the goofing around and directly speak about their discomfort. Others will demonstrate their uneasiness through nonverbal responses. When this happens, it is a good time to pause and rethink the activity. From our experience, if we have lost the ability to be safe in the group, the fun is gone as well.

## Learning From Our Mistakes

In BAM! Example, we described in detail a 10-week session with one of our boys groups that was successful. We thought it only fair to also present some examples of when things have not worked so smoothly in our groups. We offer these examples as "cautionary tales" that hopefully you can learn from in facilitating your own work with boys.

**Too Much Risk, Not Enough Support**  One particular group of boys we worked with had already been strongly influenced by a culturally conservative view regarding gender and sexual orientation. When we did the "boy in the box" activity with them, for example, they urged us to underline statements like "men should not be fags." When we tried to engage them in a discussion about how, in our view, we accepted and respected homosexuality as one of many legitimate ways of being a man, they rebelled. "Shit, what are you talking about?" one of the boys said, "Man, I'm outta this group!"

In processing this session later among ourselves, we realized that we had made two mistakes. First, we had let ourselves be pulled into a power struggle that placed us in a position of trying to change group members' views regarding homosexuality. Second, we forgot one of our basic rules (described earlier) of balancing support and risk, of making sure there was enough support for the boys in the group to take on the risks we were posing for them. In this case, asking them to accept a more liberal view of homosexuality was a huge risk for them, given how they had already learned to see their world and their role as a man within it.

Although we make it clear to the boys that we accept many ways of being male, we have learned to not put our focus on changing their views regarding sexual orientation. We do address the terms used in "gay bashing" for what they are: put-downs. We reinforce with the boys the rule that we do not accept put-downs in the group. We point out that all the names they listed that they get called when they step "outside the box" (e.g., "gay", "fag", etc.) are put-downs.

The aim of the "boy in the box" activity is to increase participants' understanding of the social pressures that they face and to come to an understanding that these social pressures can lead to unhealthy ways of being. What we have since learned is to take smaller steps with the "boy in the box" exercise, especially if we only have 10 weeks to work with a group of boys who may have very conservative views. The exercise works best when we let it unfold naturally and we let the boys come to their own conclusions by asking questions of them.

For example, an idea that regularly gets put "inside the box" is that boys shouldn't express much emotion except anger. We therefore try to help them move toward acceptance of a broader emotional repertoire by asking them such questions as: "Is it okay to cry when your pet dies?" or "Don't boys get sad too?" or "What happens to a boy who bottles things up?" We ask questions that lead them to an understanding that the limitations of the box ultimately do not serve them well.

We have learned that 10 weeks is a short period of time to introduce boys to what may be an entirely new worldview for them. We have learned to take them on this journey by starting with smaller steps. In short, we try to help them get more empathetic with themselves before pushing them to be more empathetic with others.

**Too Many Boys in Trouble** The first time we ran this group, it failed miserably. While some of the boys in that group may have benefited from the experience, we as leaders walked away thinking we would never put ourselves into such a difficult or vulnerable position again. To explain: The first time we led this group, we allowed the principal and staff at the school to fill the group with the most troubled boys at the school. Many years later, this particular group of boys who ended up in our first group is still remembered as being the most difficult set of fifth graders the school has ever had to deal with.

One boy in this group had gotten into trouble so many times that he just sat and glared at us, thinking he was in trouble all over again. Another angry boy simply (and wisely) kept challenging us week after week with the following questions: "Why are we in this group? Is it because we're in trouble?" Our basic mistake was to allow his concern to be true: All the boys were in this group because they had already been identified as "being in trouble" and we were meant to fix them in 10 short weeks. After a number of weeks during which the boys would not let go of the (sadly correct) notion that they were simply in the group because they were "in trouble," the group unraveled: One boy was suspended, another spent most of his time in the hallway outside our office because of his nastiness toward others, and a couple of other boys just stopped attending.

As young boys, we probably would have stopped coming to such a group as well. We have learned that, in terms of composition, it is very important to have the mix of boys in the group include those who are doing relatively well in school as well as those who are really struggling. We stress that BAM! groups are for every boy in the school and we try to make it something both we and they want to experience. In this way, we make it a group that everyone can benefit from.

**Being Careful About Disclosure** Another year we also had a boy who very much did not want to be in the group. In retrospect, we perhaps should have allowed him to exit the group gracefully because his later behaviors undermined the group experience for many, including us as group leaders. It happened this way: The group was meeting for the first time after the winter holidays and as part of the "check-in" the boys had been asked by the leader what they had done over the break that had been fun. When it was the leader's turn to check in, he described how over the holidays he had driven with his fiancée to visit her family in another part of the state. On hearing this disclosure, one of the boys asked in a challenging way, "Did you sleep with your girlfriend?" The leader responded, "Well, Jason, we have an adult relationship that is private and while it is okay for you to be curious about what adults do, I hope that you can respect that." The next day, we got a call from the principal of this school asking us to meet with the parent of this child, who was enraged that we would talk about sex as part of the boy's group.

A few days later, we attended an uncomfortable meeting with the principal, the parent, and the child, Jason. At this meeting, the mother stated that Jason had told her that one of the leaders had been talking "about having sex with his girlfriend," which she did not consider appropriate. She went on to say that she wanted Jason removed from the group at once. Needless to say, Jason left the group, just as he had hoped.

From this, we as leaders learned a couple of things: First, we make sure after the first session of each 10-week group that each of the boys wants to come back and be a part of what we have planned. Like our last example, we have learned that this group can only have a positive influence on boys who are open to having it. Secondly, we learned to be more thoughtful about what we share about our lives as leaders. A better response to Jason might have been, "That is something I am not willing to talk with you about." Although we recognize the curiosity that maturing boys have about sexuality, addressing sexuality is not one of our group goals.

## Dealing With Difficult Behavior

Boys behave better when expectations are clear. We present group ground rules in a way that is welcoming and invites the boys to participate. We tell them that the purpose of the rules is so that we can have fun, feel comfortable, and get a lot done. Our ground rules are few in number:

> Be respectful
> Listen to learn
> Take risks, be safe
> Honor confidentiality

Again, we are uncompromising in our efforts to create a safe environment for the boys. Group leaders must take the lead in establishing an environment free from hurtful teasing as well as homophobic and misogynist comments. We have made mistakes in the past by trying to be too "nice" with the boys, letting comments slide that we should have confronted directly. We have learned that the tougher the boys know we are on the "be respectful" rule, the more willing they are to participate in the group.

For some boys, clearly stated ground rules will be sufficient to help them manage their behavior. For others, it's not so simple. Before responding to boys' misbehavior, try to understand the cause of it. Are they bored, overly excited, lacking the social skills necessary to manage the situation, or responding to a personal vulnerability in a defensive way? Each of these hypotheses may offer a different response to the behavior.

Certain combinations of boys sitting near each other can contribute to disruptive behavior as well. In our debriefing sessions at the end of the day, we have often decided who will sit where in the next week in order to defuse certain situations. We have also had to think about engaging the boys in very particular moments of the group. For example, one week we decided that we would ask a particularly rowdy group of boys to do a drawing for us about their weekend just as they came into the room. The next week, we led the boys through a brief set of yoga postures as they entered the room. Without such an activity, the opening of our sessions had become a little to crazy for our own liking.

A common concern when BAM! groups are held during the school day is how the boys leave the group, move through the halls, and return to their regular school schedule. We are preemptive with this by reminding the boys about positive behavior as they leave the group and return to class. Because they see coming to BAM! groups as a treat, they rarely have created problems on their way back to class.

When responding to problematic behavior, it is important to balance firm and fair limit setting with positive recognition for good behavior. Group leaders must handle misbehavior without shaming, threatening, or using physical force. Try the following ideas:

- Remind members about the group rules.
- Mention that a particular behavior is disrespectful without looking at or naming a particular boy, thereby not publicly shaming him, which could create more defiance.
- Quietly move next to a disruptive boy, put your hand on the boy's shoulder, and offer a reminder of appropriate behavior.
- Change the seating arrangement to reduce disruptive behavior.
- Help boys who are on-task to directly voice their frustration to the disruptive boy.
- Distract the boys with a story, change of pace, or change of activity. Stop the activity altogether, demonstrating to the boys that they have pushed too far.

Not knowing when they have gone too far and having poor self-control are significant stumbling blocks for many boys. We give credit when we see boys exercising self-control and managing their impulsivity. It may be helpful to incorporate ways, such as some type of reward system, to recognize boys' self-control. If what seems to be driving the misbehavior is a matter of poor skill development, you may want to consider inserting some lessons to help boys develop emotional and behavioral regulation (see Appendix for additional activities).

## Women as Group Leaders

The issue of women facilitating BAM! groups is a topic of great importance because the reality is that most social service providers are women, and, therefore, those in positions to offer BAM! groups will often be female. Women have a lot to offer boys in BAM! groups and also face some unique challenges. First and foremost, it must be said that we believe women are fully capable of being effective BAM! group leaders. Emotionally fluent women have a great deal to share with boys who need more emotional fluency. In fact, many relationally skilled men have developed their emotional fluency from a woman. Some boys will also be more willing to learn from and be open with a woman, given possible histories of abuse at the hands of a man. Women also offer boys a window into the lives of girls and represent an opportunity for the boys to experience a mutually respectful relationship with a female.

That said, there are areas of BAM! group facilitation that may present unique challenges to women leaders. Challenges regarding communication styles, strategic storytelling, managing group members' behavior, and leading the physical activities are areas we explore next.

On the whole, women tend to be pursuers of emotional conversation while men tend to be avoiders. Women may sense something is bothering someone and be resolute in their efforts to have the person discuss what is upsetting them. Based on our discussion of male development in the BAM! Orientation of this guidebook, it is easy to see how being pressured to share emotions may overwhelm boys. Women may need to develop subtler and more receptive communication styles. For example, you may try placing yourself shoulder to shoulder with a boy or providing him an opportunity for physical movement to help dissipate his anxiety.

Storytelling works differently for women leading BAM! groups. Because women don't have a personal storehouse of memories about growing up as a boy, they need to look more broadly at this aspect of group leadership. Recall that the function of storytelling is to model authenticity, make abstract ideas concrete, engage the boys, and create contact. Regardless of the leader's gender, his or her honest stories of childhood invite the boys to acknowledge their own feelings and experiences.

Women can tell stories about their childhood that illustrate common dilemmas of growing up such as fitting in, changing families, and sticking up for others. They can also share stories informing boys about what it was like growing up as a girl. Women leaders can swap stories about growing up female with the boys' stories of growing up male and have the boys "teach" them about growing up male. Female leaders can share stories about the men and boys in their lives, bring in male guests to share their stories, have a group member read one of the stories included in the session-by-session instructions, or use videos that bring in authentic boys' voices. We recommend two helpful videos in which boys speak honestly about the dilemmas of growing up male: (1) *What's Up With Middle School Guys?* (Northeastern Wisconsin In-School Telecommunications) and (2) *Raising Cain* by Michael Thompson and colleagues (available online through pbs.org/opb/raisingcain).

Women can help boys find men who will serve as models for their developing masculinity. There are all types of men a boy might take as an example of the kind of man he wants to become. This person need not be someone in an official role or possessing a particular degree. Look around your community to discover to whom young boys are drawn. It may be a coach, janitor, school administrator, someone affiliated with a religious institution, or bus driver.

Another challenge for female facilitators is that group members may push behavioral limits differently with women than with men. It is important that group leaders find a method to firmly state limits with the boys. For some women that will mean cultivating a facial expression or voice tone that communicates seriousness to the boys. Other women may need to work on showing their seriousness through actions more than words. Stopping an activity, for example, rather than threatening to stop the activity can do this.

Group members may directly challenge a female leader by commenting on her gender. They might ask something like "If this is a boys group, what are you doing here?" This question is worth considering before the group begins. As a helper, it is not necessary to experience everything a person has experienced in order to be able to help him or her. Just like an individual who is not chemically dependent can effectively provide chemical dependency services, women are able to effectively run BAM! groups.

Boys tend to have a high energy level and they tend to be physical together. Women with little experience around this type of activity may find it difficult to tolerate. Again, boys do need a high degree of physicality and they also need to know the limits to their boisterous behavior. Successful BAM! leaders will allow for enough horseplay to make the setting boy-friendly. At the same time they find ways to direct that energy toward BAM! goals. Along those lines, some of the challenges in BAM! groups require a high level of physical participation on the part of the leader. If this is uncomfortable for you, consider altering the activity or involving another adult during those activities.

Regardless of the gender, the most important qualities of BAM! group facilitators are that they fully commit to the boys, work to understand the dilemmas boys face, and authentically and playfully engage with group members. Women may possess each of these qualities. To close this section on women as leaders of BAM! groups, we offer these reflections from Monica, a female colleague of ours:

> At first, I was concerned about being a woman and facilitating a group for boys because I felt their experiences were too different from mine. However, while running a BAM! group, I learned that the boys respected me and my ideas and valued having a caring adult—male or female—invest time in them and their stories. I found it very helpful to begin the group with a discussion about the dynamics of having a female leader and to gather the boys' advice about how to make the group a success. I expected that the boys would be resistant to participating in the BAM! activities, but they enjoyed the curriculum and embraced each challenge it brought. I found the physical activities were a necessity for my boys' group, as they were fun, engaging, and educational. They gave the boys an opportunity to capture and expend their energy in a positive way while providing crucial teachable moments about how to be in the outside world. I encourage women to facilitate a boys' empowerment group and to utilize the tools offered in the BAM! curriculum!

## Men as Group Leaders

If women tend to be pursuers of emotional conversation, men tend to be avoiders. Leading a BAM! group may be difficult for men who don't make good contact themselves. For the very reasons boys need BAM! groups, men may find leading BAM! groups to be a stretch. Men generally lack role models of other relationally competent men. Additionally, men tend to devalue what they have to offer in relationships, often relegating that responsibility to women. The result is a lack of men in positions likely to offer BAM! groups.

We need to apply effort to recruit men. Men can be motivated to do this work through education about boys' difficulties. Often when men stop to look at the challenges boys face and consider their potential influence on boys, they step up to support boys. There are growing examples of men who are stepping into positions to help boys grow into healthy men.

Boys look to men as models of what it means to be a man. Men model masculinity by what they say or don't say and by how they act or don't act. Men must be especially cognizant of the subtle and not-so-subtle messages of manliness they communicate to the boys. The personal stories we choose to tell say a lot about our ideas of what is acceptable for men. For example, we may believe that a "real man" would not walk away from a fight. If so, we might feel uncomfortable telling a story about such a scenario. To add to the complexity, if we did tell that story we may covertly communicate our discomfort in how we handled the situation.

Ideas about gender are so embedded in our worldview that it can be difficult to see our own limiting ideas of what it means to be a man. A co-leader or supervisor can assist us to more honestly acknowledge our beliefs about gender. When we lead BAM! groups, we discuss our reactions to the boys after each session to stay aware of the influence of our own beliefs. If we feel a particularly intense response to a member (such as strong irritation), we consider if our reaction stems from a limiting notion *we* have about what it means to be a male.

For example, one day in our group, "Peacock Paul" wanted to demonstrate a ballet dance during the session. We felt particularly annoyed by his showiness but outwardly tolerated it. Would we have reacted the same way had he offered to demonstrate something he learned in football? We need to be careful about any messages we send to boys that limit their full expression. This care applies to other points on the continuum of maleness as well. It has to be as acceptable for boys to hunt and play football as it is for them to dance ballet and knit. Our behavior as leaders speaks volumes about what we think a man should be and do.

## Session-by-Session Instructions

In the opening to BAM! Instructions, we laid out some of the nuts and bolts to beginning a BAM! group, and we looked at the role that facilitators play. The remainder of this section provides facilitator instructions to replicate the specific activities of each BAM! group session, weeks 1 through 10. We offer these details as a guide for you to use when leading your own BAM! group. These specifics reflect how we did the activities. You may make modifications that work better for your leadership style, the tone of the group, and the physical environment in which your group takes place.

# Week 1: Lost in the Woods

This first week the boys get to know one another, learn about the group goals and rules, and face their first challenge together, the Electric Fence.

## Session Objectives

- To explain the purpose of BAM! groups

The boys will leave this session with a basic understanding of the group goals and of how time will be spent in the group.

- To model appropriate group sharing

The boys will see from the beginning that the group is a safe place to express themselves. The facilitator story will model the sharing of vulnerable feelings or unpleasant experiences, setting the standard for risk taking in the group.

- To establish a context of cooperation

The boys will understand today that they will be required to cooperate with and support one another. Help to motivate the boys by explaining that successfully demonstrating cooperative skills will allow them to advance to riskier challenges.

- To establish rules and guidelines for group behavior

The boys and adult leaders will arrive at agreed-upon group rules. Establishing rules right away and obtaining group buy-in are extremely important for creating a safe space.

- To have fun

The boys will leave this first day knowing that the group setting is fun. The first session sets the tone for the following sessions. Be sure to allow enough time for the group challenge and invest plenty of energy and excitement into its facilitation.

## What You Need

Large piece of chart paper/butcher paper with group name written in large letters

Crayons/markers/colored pencils
Foam safety mat 4 × 6 feet and at least 1.5 inches thick
Rope or string (5 feet long, with a place to tie/tape each end)
A childhood story that highlights some of the issues that boys face
Light snack (optional)

## What You Do

**The Name Game Activity (10 Minutes)**   Make contact with each boy as he arrives. Direct boys to the markers, crayons, and chart paper in the center of the group space. Ask each boy to think of a word that describes him. The first letter of the word should be the same as the first letter of his name (e.g., Guitar Pickin' Peter, Helpin' Howard, Skateboardin' Stephen). Instruct the boys to draw or write the alliterative phrase on the chart paper. Write your name(s) as well.

Once everyone has chosen a name, develop a clapping rhythm. Each boy says his alliterative name and the group echoes the name in time with the clapping (e.g., Peter says, "Pickin' Peter." Group claps twice. Then the group says "Pickin' Peter" and then group claps twice more, and so on around the circle).

**Keep in Mind...**   Look out for boys who do not seem to have friendships within the group. Make an extra effort to help them to feel comfortable. Boys may have a difficult time thinking of a name that suits them. In these cases, encourage other group members to offer some suggestions, taking care to ensure that offered names are not used as put-downs.

**Describe BAM! Groups (10 Minutes)**   Introduce yourself and describe your hopes for the group. Give the boys a brief overview of the concerns for boys (declining academic achievement, male violence, teasing). Say something similar to the following:

> We think that boys at your age are learning to be really competitive and aggressive with each other, but that you don't really get a chance to be supportive and cooperative together. Boys learn early in life to use put-downs and act like they don't care about a lot of important things, but here in this group we want to give you a chance to practice making friends and being part of a team that works together, faces challenges, and has fun. How does that sound?

Describe what will happen in the group over the next 10 weeks (challenge activities, share stories, final outing).

**Create Group Rules (5 Minutes)**   Generate a list of rules or expectations that will support both physical and emotional safety in the group. Allow other rules to be added if participants have suggestions. A potential list of rules might include:

No put-downs

One person speaks at a time (identify a talking stick/object)

The right to pass

Confidentiality

Honesty

Be open to learn

Once the expectations are established, obtain verbal agreement that everyone is willing to follow them. Discuss how group members can respectfully remind one another of the rules when they are broken.

**Keep in Mind...** Be vigilant about violations of the rules, using such occasions as opportunities for practicing problem-solving skills and positive communication. The group must be a safe place. See the earlier section on Dealing with Difficult Behavior for more ideas.

**Facilitator Story (15 Minutes)** Tell a detailed story about your childhood that illustrates some of the challenges that boys face. Describe the feelings that you had at the time and the lessons that you learned. If you cannot think of an appropriate story, or if you feel uncomfortable sharing one that comes to mind, consider having one of the boys in the group read one of the stories below for discussion.

### Facilitator Story 1: "Run, Howie, Run!"

I was about 10 years old. I was always a poor athlete, a little slow, husky, and uncoordinated. I struck out most times at bat in little league. Mostly kids liked me anyway because I was a good team supporter.

One time we were playing at the field at Sharp Corners School, and I came up to bat and swung . . . but nobody could find the ball! My coach started yelling, "Run, Howie, run!" I got to first base and paused while the outfielders, infielders, and the other team's coaches were looking around for the ball. Still no ball! Each base I got to . . . 2nd, 3rd. The same thing! I would pause, but still there was no ball! Now the fans were yelling at me to keep running. Everyone was involved. Eventually, they waved me home and I scored. Moments later, the opposing coach found the ball caught underneath the catcher's chest protector!

I remember having a mix of feelings that day. I was happy that I scored, but I was also sort of humiliated that it had happened that way. Still, everyone got a good laugh out of it. I wanted to tell you this story because I know not all of you are great athletes, and I wanted you to know that I wasn't a great athlete either. But I did have a sense of humor and kids liked me for that. What I imagine is that each of you has special strengths and talents that we will get to see as our group goes on over the next few weeks.

### Facilitator Story 2: "Leave Him Alone!"

I grew up in New York. In the fifth grade, I played on a Little League team with lots of my friends. The league was split into six teams and I had friends on several of those teams, but the majority of my friends were on my own team. We were the Tigers, and my friend Jeffrey Ferrara played on the Lions. He was their pitcher and the Lions were the best team in the league. Jeffrey was very athletic, but a little shy. He was a great pitcher.

On this day, we had a game against the Lions, and Jeffrey was pitching. For some reason, Jeffrey was not having a good day at the mound, and we were hitting a lot of his pitches. It was clear that Jeffrey was shaken by the hits, and my team decided to take advantage of this. They started chanting, "We want a pit-cher, not a belly-itcher!" If Jeffrey was rattled before, he was really shaken now. He was looking more and more like he might cry as my teammates yelled louder and louder, "We want a pit-cher, not a belly-itcher!"

Because Jeffrey was my friend, I felt really bad for him. I wanted to win the game, but not at the expense of my friend's humiliation. When I couldn't watch or listen any more, I stood up on the bench behind my teammates and yelled, "Leave him alone! That's enough, you guys! That's enough!" My teammates and coach looked at me like I was crazy, but they did stop chanting.

That was my last season playing organized sports, but Jeffrey was still my friend. I think I told you this story because it says a little bit about the conflicts that I faced as a boy and that I think most boys face. They want to be friends with each other, but sometimes they are almost forced to be really mean to each other. In this group, I hope we can face some challenges together as a team where we can also be friends with each other afterward.

### Facilitator Story 3: "Foul Ball!"

I used to strike out so much in baseball in the fifth grade that the kids in my class used to call me the "strikeout king." Then one day, I really connected with the ball in a big game with a neighboring school. I watched the ball curve high over the third baseman's head and land on the chalk line in deep left field, sending up a plume of white chalk dust. It wasn't until after I had excitedly rounded first base and was on my way to second base that I heard the umpire yelling "Foul!" and the boys on the other team were telling me to stop running.

I immediately started crying in front of everyone because I felt it was so unfair that the ball had been called foul. I also felt really angry at the umpire, and, on top of all that, I felt embarrassed to be seen crying by all the boys on both teams. I guess I was an emotional kid.

**Electric Fence Activity (20 Minutes)**   Fasten a string or a rope across the middle of the group space, approximately 4 feet high. Position the safety mat underneath the rope so that there is an equal portion of mat on either side of the rope. Instruct group members to take off their shoes and to all stand on the same side of the rope. Tell the following story:

You are all lost in the woods! You have been lost for 3 days without any food other than the grubs you have found under logs and you have had no water except for the dew you have collected from leaves in the morning. You are hungry and thirsty and you each have 5 bucks in your pockets that you would love to spend on a hamburger and a milkshake somewhere.

Suddenly, after 3 long days, you come to the edge of the forest and, lo and behold, right across the meadow is a Burgerville! You rush to get to it, but one of you jumps back with a shriek, getting shocked by an electric fence standing between you and your first burger all week!

Your challenge as a group is the following: You must get everyone in your group safely over this electric fence. There are a few rules: No one can touch or go under the fence. You may not throw anyone over the fence and you must stay in physical contact with the person going over the fence at all times. Be gentle. Oh look! Here are some kindly farmers [facilitators] to help you. Now take a few moments to plan how you will get everyone over the fence safely.

Give the boys a few minutes prior to attempting the challenge to plan for how they will proceed.

Position one facilitator on either side of the rope. If there is only one facilitator, begin on the opposite side of the rope from the boys to assist with the first few crossing over. When several boys have crossed over, switch to the other side of the rope and help the remainder of the boys to cross (provide some explanation as to your "magical" ability to pass through the fence).

**Debriefing the Activity**  When the boys have finished with the activity, ask questions about how it felt to be supported: Did the boys goof around or did someone get hurt? Ask individuals if it felt like the group was serious about their safety. If boys are able to acknowledge feeling unsafe, ask what they would like from the group in the future. Facilitators should offer their own observations about the group's performance, identifying strengths and areas for growth. Were the boys careful and focused on one another's safety? If so, praise them for taking care of one another. If the boys were particularly careless, consider trying the activity again the following week. Avoid shaming the group, but acknowledge the need to practice more before attempting riskier challenges.

**Evaluations**  Pass out copies of the pretest portion of the group evaluations (refer to the Appendix for a copy of the pre-evaluation). Explain the directions in detail and answer any questions about the test before allowing the boys to begin. Collect the pretests when the boys are done and put them in a file to be compared with completed posttests from the last session of the group.

**Closing (10 Minutes)**  Go around the circle and ask the boys to say one word that describes how they feel about the group so far. Ask how many of the boys are willing to commit to the full 10 weeks of the group. Give the boys who are uncertain one more week to decide.

**Keep in Mind...**  Boys are often energized and wound up after the group. If you are in a school or another structured environment, remind them to walk to their next destination, keeping their voices low and respecting others that might be working.

## Week 2: Alligator Swamp

This week, boys learn about one another through telling their 60-Second Autobiographies, discussing the importance of controlling impulses, and facing the perilous Alligator Swamp together.

## Session Objectives

- To improve impulse control

Boys will leave this group session with an understanding of why impulse control is important and with an awareness of their own ability/challenges with thinking before acting.

- To build group cohesiveness

Boys will get to know one another better by discovering their differences and similarities.

- To practice active listening

Boys will practice active listening by giving good attention to the person sharing his 60-Second Autobiography.

## What You Need

A layout on the floor of the Xs and swamp parameters

A map of the path through the swamp

A childhood story for telling

## What You Do

**Opening (5 Minutes)**   Mark boys' attendance with a star by their names on the group poster and welcome them each individually. Review the highlights of the previous week.

**60-Second Autobiography (10 Minutes)**   In this brief activity, ask each boy to talk about himself for 60 seconds, sharing anything he feels is important. Instruct boys on either side of the speaker to report one thing that they learned about the speaker from his story. Begin by telling your own autobiography, modeling the types of things that might be shared: place of birth, age, interests, pastimes, friends, special skills, and so forth. Allow two or three group members to share. The rest will share next week. Listen for the sharing of more sensitive information. Acknowledge boys for taking the risk of sharing such information with the group.

**Keep in Mind...**   In the early stages of this group, emphasis is placed on establishing relationships and group identity. The autobiographies help group members to get to know one another, and the listening task associated with it supports mutual respect. Commonalities between group members are identified when similar stories and experiences are shared (e.g., divorce, trouble with impulsivity, etc.). Successful completion of each challenge is always an opportunity for supporting unity in the group, praising the cooperation and support utilized.

The 60-Second Autobiography activity is the first chance that boys have to talk about themselves at any length. Boys may have difficulty filling the entire 60 seconds. If so, encourage the listeners to ask questions or simply move on.

Boys may fail to listen when it is not their turn or stop listening when they or their friends have finished. Limit side conversations and efforts to steal attention. Allow questions/comments from group members that keep attention focused on the speaker. Be sure to respectfully reengage boys as listeners when they lose focus.

**Facilitator Story (15 Minutes)**    Prepare a story to tell about your childhood that relates to this session's theme: impulse control. Describe the feelings that you had at the time, the consequences of your actions, and the lessons that you learned. If you do not have an appropriate story, use the one below:

### Facilitator Story: "Sheep Head"

In the fourth grade, I went to a school in Washington State where teachers were very strict. I had several friends there, but often felt like I did not fit in because I was the only black kid in the school. One kid in particular, Brandon Sooner, liked to tease me about my "sheep head." Finally I had had enough. One day, when he called me "sheep head" from across the classroom so that everyone could hear, I picked up the nearest object (an apple) and hurled it at Brandon. Brandon moved out of the way, and the apple shattered a huge window, scattering glass everywhere.

Looking back, I remember being scared about the spanking I was sure to get from the principal, but I'm sure that I would have felt worse if Brandon had been hurt. I was right to be angry, but I had handled it in a way that might really have hurt Brandon or anyone standing near the window. It was a good lesson for me that day to calm down and think before acting on my feelings. I did get a spanking, but the principal also made sure that no one ever called me "sheep head" again.

Ask boys to go around and briefly share a time that acting without thinking got them into trouble. Acknowledge that each of us has trouble with acting without thinking. Encourage boys to help each other with this respectfully, both inside of the group and outside. Next, help the boys understand that the next activity they will do, described as follows, is also about thinking before acting.

**Alligator Swamp Activity (30 Minutes)**    Ask participants to stand behind a length of tape signifying the edge of the swamp. Tell the following story:

You are on an expedition in the Everglades, searching for buried pirate treasure. According to your map, the treasure is just on the other side of an alligator swamp. The only way to get across is by stepping on each of the alligator heads without waking them. However, there is a specific path that you must follow to avoid waking the extremely hungry alligators. Learn and memorize the path, and you all will make it across. If someone steps incorrectly, he must run quickly to the end of the line to avoid being eaten by the wakened gator. You may help each other to remember the path by making hand gestures, but you must remain absolutely silent while your friends are crossing or the gators will wake up. Good luck!

The boys face a grid of *X*s taped to the floor in rows, three by three (easier) or four by four (harder). In a sequence unknown to the group members, each *X* represents exactly one footstep along the path to the other side of the swamp (see example). A single *X* will never be stepped on more than once, and boys will never need to jump over an *X* to pick up the trail. Stepping on an *X* in the appropriate sequence elicits a "DING" from the leader. An incorrect step (or any noises from participants) elicits a "RAAAAAWR" from the leader, indicating the awakening of the deadly alligators and the potential devouring of the boy in the swamp (he goes to the end of the line for another try). Participants must discover and walk the entire path through a process of trial and error, remembering correct and incorrect steps of the sequence. Boys may help each other along the way by pointing or gesturing to appropriate *X*s. The activity is over once all boys have gotten to the other side. See graphic below for an example of a swamp map.

*Alligator Swamp Diagram*

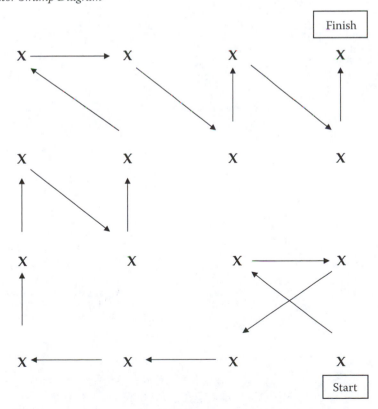

**Debriefing the Activity**    Ask the group about the experience that they had with the activity. Comment on the performance of the group, making connections to the earlier conversation about impulse control. If someone showed particular difficulty with this during the activity, talk about how we each have different things we are good at and this may not be something everyone is good at. Ask about how it was to get help from others. Particularly appreciate those who disclose serious troubles with impulse control when they perform well on this task.

**Keep in Mind...**    The Alligator Swamp is an exciting activity that offers a chance to practice slowing down and thinking in order to avoid mistakes. Group participants who show marked difficulty with controlling impulses (e.g., making mistakes from going too fast, failing to listen to the advice of their peers) get feedback from their peers about their impulsivity and how it affects others. See the Additional Activities section for another idea about how to speak with the boys about impulse control.

## Week 3: Haunted House

This week, the boys learn that it is okay to admit to feeling afraid after facing the Haunted House.

## Session Objectives

- To normalize the expression of fear

Participants will leave this session with a beginning understanding of social forces that make it difficult for boys to be honest about feeling afraid. They will also leave having experienced the group to be a place where being honest about fear will be accepted and supported.

- To build group cohesion

Boys strengthen their relationships with one another by cooperating to complete a scary challenge. Boys will build trust and earn trust as all group members assume responsibility for one another's safety.

## What You Need

Cloth blindfolds for each group member

A prepared story that describes the Haunted House activity

Prior communication with school staff/relevant others about venturing outside of the group space

Noisemakers and props for the Haunted House

## What You Do

**60-Second Autobiography (10 Minutes)**   Finish this activity by allowing those boys who did not get a chance last week to tell their stories. Refer to the instructions from last week to facilitate this activity.

**Haunted House Activity (50 Minutes)**   Prepare your environment to reflect the haunted elements of your story. You might enlist helpers to make noises and facilitate spooky effects. Devise a story similar to the following that explains some type of unsolved, supernatural occurrence, tailoring the details to fit your group setting (i.e., school layout/grounds):

> I need to tell you guys that there is something in the basement of this school. It has been there all week. Yesterday one of the staff went down to solve the problem and he hasn't come back yet. Some people heard a few loud screams and there are also some kinds of weird electrical problems happening all over the school. We weren't going to tell you about it, none of the other kids at school know, but the principal asked us to talk to you as a group. At the last faculty meeting the principal

asked if anyone could come up with any ideas on what to do about the thing in the basement. Someone mentioned it might be a good job for the fifth-grade boys group. We think you guys are ready for this challenge, but it's not going to be easy.

Here's what we know. We know this thing will kill you if you look at it directly. We also know that you will die if it finds you alone. So here's the plan: We are going to need to blindfold each of you so you can't see the monster. But you can hold on to the arm of the boy in front of you. In fact you will need to hold on to him if you want to survive. Remember, if it finds you alone, it's over for you. We also know that this thing might be chased off if we use a particular chant that seems to have worked at other schools. We will lead you all the way down into the basement and there you will have to perform the chant perfectly. We will show you how to do the chant now.

Instruct the boys to line up, help them put on their blindfolds, and tell them to place their left hands on the shoulder of the person in front of them. Lead the boys through the haunted environment, accounting for their safety while blindfolded. When the boys reach the final destination, instruct them to get in a circle with hands on top of each other in the middle. Perform the practiced chant and indicate to the boys that the challenge is complete. Return to the group space to process the experience.

**Debriefing the Activity**   Ask the boys how it was for them to do this activity and what they felt while doing it. Encourage the boys to share all feelings associated with the activity. Acknowledge the courage that it takes to share vulnerability with other boys. Appreciate any encouragement or support that boys offered to each other throughout the day. Regardless of whether or not the boys believed the story, highlight again the cooperation used to complete the task. Inevitably, there will be those who disclaim the validity of the story or deny feeling nervous or afraid. This is perfectly fine. Once one or two admit to feeling afraid, others generally follow.

**Keep in Mind...**   If someone seems particularly frightened, take him aside or remove his blindfold to tell him secretly that the story is make-believe. Although fear is a part of this activity, the goal is not to terrify the boys. We want to provide them with an exciting group challenge, without compromising their feelings of safety.

# Week 4: Sitting Circle

This week, boys reveal more of themselves by way of the family stories and complete a fun cooperative activity called the Sitting Circle.

## Session Objectives

- To build group cohesion

The boys will reveal themselves more fully to the group by sharing about their families. They will learn that other boys have family struggles similar to their own. They will experience the safety of talking about family without being judged and the acceptance of the group communicated through focused attention.

- To practice active listening

The boys will offer focused attention to others in the group for a significant portion of the session's time.

## Things You Need

Foam safety mat

A personal family story that illustrates some of your family relationships

## What You Do

### OPENING (10 MINUTES)

Reflect on last week's activity, catching up any boys who may have been absent and allowing any unsaid comments to be made. Highlight last week's focus on fear and reissue praise for those who were willing to admit fear to the group. Provide an opportunity for those boys who have not yet had the chance to tell their 60-Second Autobiography.

### FACILITATOR STORY (10 MINUTES)

Prepare a story or description that covers the range of your family experience: relationship to parents/caregivers and siblings, parents' relationship with each other, enjoyable times, stressful experiences, lessons learned, and so forth. If you do not have an appropriate story available, use the one below:

**Facilitator Story: "Family Story"**

I want to tell you guys a story about what I learned with my family. My dad didn't take good care of himself. He had a stressful job where he dealt with lots of racism, so when he got home he drank lots of alcohol and ate unhealthy but satisfying food. He worked hard and loved us, but he ended up getting very sick and he eventually died from a stroke. That happened when I was only one and a half, so I did not get to spend much time with my father, but I learned quite a bit from him. My father worked hard, and he was able to get an education and a good job at a time when bad schools for black people and racism made it difficult for black men to be successful. I am proud of his accomplishments, and I am reminded of how believing in yourself and not giving up can help you to achieve huge goals.

I also learned from my father about how men have a hard time dealing with their feelings. Instead of sharing his feelings with my mom, my father kept them inside, using alcohol to try to keep the feelings away. The result was that my father passed away far too early, leaving my brother and me to learn the hard way about how important it is for a man to deal with difficult feelings in positive ways. We were raised instead by our mother and grandmother, who did a great job of teaching us about what it means to be men. Now that I have my own children, I want to take better care of myself than my dad did of himself so that I can be around for my two boys as they grow up.

**Keep in Mind...**   This story should be chosen wisely, taking into account exactly what details you are willing to share and why. Be aware of your personal feelings associated with the experience. You must be prepared to contain your own emotions as well as the feelings that the story may evoke in the boys.

**Family Stories (25 Minutes)**   Before beginning this activity, remind the boys of group expectations for respect and confidentiality. Give the boys a few minutes each to share about their own families. If they have trouble identifying things to share, however, guide them with a few questions or directives (e.g., With whom do you live? Say one thing that you like about your family and one thing that you dislike. With whom do you get along best/worst in your family? What does your family like to do together?). Keep attention focused on the sharer, but allow others to make comments about the story (not diverting attention from the speaker).

Look for similarities between stories and build connections between group members by highlighting commonalities. Acknowledge group members for taking the risk of sharing sensitive information. Encourage group members to make supportive comments to one another.

**Keep in Mind...**   It is unlikely that everyone will have the chance in one day to share his story. Allow some time in the next session for boys to share their family stories if they have not yet had the chance.

**The Sitting Circle Activity (15 Minutes)**   Instruct group members to stand in a tight circle, shoulder to shoulder. Next, ask the boys to turn their bodies 45° to the right so that they are all still in a circle facing the back of the person that is in front of them. Once in this position, ask boys to take one side-step to the left toward the center of the circle. It is important that the group is now very close with little space left between their shoulders in the inside of the circle. The object of this challenge is for all group members to simultaneously sit down on the knees of the person behind them such that everyone is sitting in a circle. When the boys are in the correct standing position, instruct them to slowly and gently sit down on the person's knees behind them on the count of three.

**Keep in Mind...** It typically takes boys a few times to complete the task, adjusting their bodies and synchronizing their sit. Boys have fun with this task because it is physical and provides an opportunity to make contact with one another. Remind them, though, that despite its lacking risk, the activity is a cooperative pretest for riskier challenges to come. Encourage the boys to communicate and give focus toward successfully and cooperatively completing the task.

## Week 5: Willow in the Wind

This week, the boys begin to explore the power that teasing has on their behavior, and they take greater physical and emotional risks by way of the Willow in the Wind challenge.

## Session Objectives

- To understand the powerful effects of teasing

Boys will understand the way that teasing can change the behavior of the person being teased, even to the point of abandoning personal characteristics or interests that the individual likes or appreciates about himself (e.g., a boy cuts his long hair because he is teased about it).

- To build group cohesion

Boys will increase their level of trust for other group members. The Willow in the Wind activity can be frightening for boys because they must trust that their teammates will support them physically and that they will not shame them for their fear.

- To expand the boys' emotional repertoire

Boys are asked to describe the many feelings and sensations associated with the challenge activity. Boys have difficulty admitting to feeling afraid that they might be dropped. They receive coaching and support from the group to express the range of emotions associated with this activity.

## What You Need

Blindfold

Foam safety mat

Chart paper (or use the back of your banner) and markers

A story about a time when you were teased or when you teased someone else

## What You Do

**Opening (10 Minutes)**    Ask each boy to choose a weather system to describe how he is feeling today (e.g., calm, stormy, etc.).

**Facilitator Story (15 Minutes)**    Prepare and tell a story that describes a time when being teased by other kids influenced you to change yourself to avoid the teasing. Use the following story as a backup in case you do not have one of your own:

**Facilitator Story: "The Pink Shirt"**

I went to junior high in the mid-80s in Brooklyn. In the seventh grade, I had one shirt that I was particularly fond of, a pink polo shirt that I wore with the collar turned up. This pink shirt became the excuse for a group of boys to pick a fight with me.

Anthony Grazzle started it. I think he did it because he was the smallest guy in his group and he needed to "prove himself." He walked up to me in gym class and called me gay for wearing the pink shirt.

I didn't hit Anthony, but I stood up and got in his face. Then he hit me and I hit him back. Before I knew it, a group of his friends were holding me while Anthony punched and kicked me. I still can't believe that the P.E. teacher never saw what happened. Everyone knew that an unresolved fight would be settled "after school." In fact, I think Anthony said those very words to me as we were separating.

A crowd gathered after school, expecting to relocate to a place that was far enough away to not get caught by adults. I was really nervous and thought seriously about going home, but I was almost more afraid of what might happen if I did not show up. I worried that people would think I was chicken, and that other boys would pick on me even more. Feeling like I had no choice, I went to face Anthony, hoping that at least one of my friends would tell me that he would still respect me if I did not go, maybe respect me more. I did not receive this support.

I learned a few things from that experience: I learned about being teased. I learned about how boys sometimes feel as though they have to stick up for themselves, being pushed to fight even when they don't want to. I learned that it is not always easy to be a boy. That it feels sometimes like you have to do things that you don't want to do in order for people to like and respect you.

Now I want to be very clear. I am not saying that I think that boys should fight in order to be accepted by their friends. I don't want you to fight at all. What I want is for you to know that the adults in this room understand how scary it can be to choose not to fight, how the fear that losing friends or getting picked on even more is real. Our hope, though, is that you will see that there are friends out there, like the ones that you have in this group, who will support you in staying out of fights, and who will not tease you for being different.

**Teasing Discussion (15 Minutes)**   Ask the boys to list the things about which they or others have been teased. Write these things on a large piece of chart paper. Take extra care to support boys as they share these vulnerable experiences. Encourage group members to make supportive comments to one another about their experiences with teasing, supporting one another by relating similar experiences and showing understanding. Take notice of common themes that seem to emerge from the teasing list. Explain that we will make some new lists next week that closely relate to the topic of teasing.

**Willow in the Wind Activity (20 Minutes)**   Have the boys stand in a tight circle shoulder to shoulder surrounding an individual standing on a safety mat in the middle. Arms crossed against his chest, the person in the middle leans, stiff-bodied in various directions, trusting that the boys in the ring will use their hands to keep him from falling. The option is given to the leaner as to whether or not he would like to be blindfolded for the activity.

Because safety is an issue, have the boys practice this leaning activity in pairs before actually attempting the group challenge. Demonstrate and coach the boys to use a supportive leg stance (one foot forward with the knee bent; the other foot planted behind with the leg straight). Show the boys how to support the "leaner" with their hands, holding their hands up, level with their chest, palms outward with arms slightly bent. Palm against palm, one boy leans into the other, giving the other the practice of supporting.

Once the dyads demonstrate that they have the skill, ask them to form a circle and establish an order of turns. Instruct the boys to form a tight circle, shoulder to shoulder. There should be no gaps between boys through which someone could fall. Ask the boys to plant their front foot, one foot away from the person in the middle. Their palms should also extend one foot from the middle person's body, and boys should be instructed to keep their hands raised at all times (even when a person is not falling in their direction). The rule about supporting the leaner is that regardless of which direction he goes, three boys should have hands on him each time.

Instruct the person in the middle to cross his arms over his chest and to keep his body stiff as a board. Coach him to flex each muscle in his body to keep stiff, reminding him that it is more difficult to support a floppy body than a stiff body. The leaner is in complete control of when he falls, asking the group if they are ready to catch him and telling them that he is ready to fall when they respond in the affirmative. The leaner also controls the direction in which he falls (instruct boys in the ring to gently push the leaner back to the middle of the circle, but not to push him to fall in a different direction).

After several successful catches, indicate to the boys that the final lean should be straight back, and instruct the entire group to gently lower the leaner toward the ground. When the leaner's upper torso is lowered to approximately 45°, instruct the boys around the circle to move in and use their hands to support the leaner's head, back, legs, and feet. Once everyone has taken a position, instruct the boys at the legs and feet to lift the leaner's legs and feet to be level with the leaner's torso and head. In other words, the legs and feet will be lifted to completely suspend the boy horizontally above the ground. Once the boy is horizontal, instruct the boys to lift the suspended boy up, over everyone's heads. Ask everyone to be absolutely silent. Suspend the boy in the air for a count of five or more in complete silence, and then gently lower him to the mat. Depending on the level of focus, make a choice about whether or not you should join the circle to support and lift the leaner.

**Debriefing the Activity**   Ask the boys how it felt to do this activity. What was it like to be the leaner? What was it like to be the supporter? Group focus with this activity almost always falters a little. Encourage dialogue about how lacking focus jeopardized the safety of group members. When appropriate, encourage group members to make direct requests of focus from those who are goofing off. Ultimately, the goal is to discuss how the cooperation of many made the success of this activity possible. If you did not need to assist, use this point to praise the group's performance and to build unity.

**Keep in Mind…** Be very firm about behavior during this activity to ensure the safety of the leaners. If focus breaks down too often, too long, or in any major ways, consider postponing the completion of the activity until the group demonstrates readiness to try it. This is a "challenge by choice" activity where boys may choose whether or not they would like to fall and/or be lifted. No choice, however, is given about supporting the leaners. Each boy is expected to help with this. If some boys elect not to try the leaning or to be lifted, be sure to praise them at the end of the activity, citing the courage it takes to make choices that are different from that of the group.

## Week 6: Making Lists

This week, the boys learn about social influences on male behavior and identity and the consequences that result when boys fail to behave in expected ways.

## Session Objectives

- To learn about male socialization

Boys will leave this session with an understanding of how teasing and shaming often force boys to give up parts of themselves and to behave in ways that are personally and socially destructive. The group examines the ways that social messages about masculinity confine boys to a limited set of behaviors and feelings.

- To expand the boys' emotional repertoire

Boys will go further today with the discussion about teasing, discussing the ways that boys are teased when they do not go along with expectations for men and boys. Boys list the names that boys are called and explain how being called those names makes them feel.

## What You Need

Foam safety mat
Blindfold
Chart paper and markers
A personal story about having been teased for behaving differently from what is socially acceptable for men and boys

## What You Do

**Opening (5 Minutes)**    Ask each boy to describe something about himself that he likes or is proud of.

**Facilitator Story (10 Minutes)**    Tell a story that describes a time when you went against social expectations for boys ("outside the box") despite the inevitability of being teased. Describe the outcome and, particularly, how it impacted your thoughts and behavior. Use the following story if you need to:

### Facilitator Story: "What's *She* Doing Here?!"

When I was about 15 years old I had a paper route. Every day I would fold my papers, stuff them in my shoulder bags, and then ride around my neighborhood delivering them to all the houses on my route. One Friday afternoon, I was delivering my papers and thinking about a party I was going to have on Saturday night at my house. I had invited some of my friends and we were going to play ping-pong, play music, and eat lots of food.

I was thinking about this party when I threw a paper into the driveway of Terry Walford's house. Terry was a girl in my class who was different than the rest of us. She kind of looked and walked funny and she didn't have any real friends at school at all. As I threw the paper, I saw her walking around the yard of her house by herself, and I realized how lonely she must be. I decided that I would invite her to my party.

Terry was really happy to be invited to the party and she was the first one to arrive the next night at my house. When my other friends showed up, one of them, Wally Jeffries, gave me a weird look when he saw Terry. Then he said, loud enough for everyone to hear, "Sick! What's *she* doing here?!" When I told him that I had invited her, I half expected him to leave the party. Maybe I just hoped that he would leave. But he ended up staying anyway and so did Terry. I remember feeling uncomfortable during the party about having invited Terry, but I also felt kind of proud too.

Describe how the story relates to established social expectations for boys' behavior.

**The Boy in the Box Activity (25 Minutes)**   Ask the boys to generate a list of the social expectations and pressures that they experience. Refer to last week's session about teasing to frame this activity. Write boys' responses on a large sheet of butcher paper, hung where everyone can see. On the paper, draw a large box in which you will write their responses.

Next, ask the boys to create a new list of the types of names that boys get called when they act differently from the box (e.g., when boys are not tough or strong). Finally, ask boys to talk about the effects of being called these names. The following prompt is given as an example:

> When we are called these names or when we worry about being called these names, how does it change the way that we might normally behave?

**Keep in Mind...**   The list they generate might have pro-social boy behaviors (e.g., being loyal or athletic) as well as limiting behaviors (e.g., only showing anger or getting into trouble). It is important that part of their list contain some of the limiting messages boys receive. If boys have difficulty thinking of some of those qualities, have them think of a popular media figure (e.g., Bart Simpson or Eminem) and have them list the messages that those figures send boys about what a boy is supposed to be like. Give specific examples if group members are offtrack.

**Willow in the Wind Activity (20 Minutes)**   It is likely that a few boys have not yet had the chance to do the Willow in the Wind activity. Give them the opportunity to complete the activity here. Please refer to week 5 for instructions on this activity's procedure and process.

## Week 7: Treasure Hunt

This week, the boys embark on the Treasure Hunt where they face physical challenges, appreciate one another for their individual strengths, and identify personal characteristics or preferences that go beyond the typical social expectations for men.

## Session Objectives

- To increase boys' connections to one another

The boys will receive appreciations from other group members and the facilitators. In receiving those appreciations, we notice significant improvements in the boys' sense of connections to other individuals in the group. In giving the appreciations, boys practice their skills with direct, positive communication.

- To improve focus

The boys will have practice remaining focused in the midst of a very physical activity.

- To expand the definition of manhood

The boys will receive validation and support from other group members for having personal characteristics that go beyond the box.

- To learn about supportive friendships

The boys will consider what it means to have a truly supportive friendship. The facilitator story illustrates to boys how positive friendships provide the kind of support that allows boys to resist peer pressure and to be who they are without shame. The appreciations activity provides an example of how this type of support strengthens us.

## What You Need

The entire treasure hunt mapped out and prepared

A treat to serve as the "treasure"

A story about a time when a friend supported you for being "outside the box"

## What You Do

**Facilitator Story (10 Minutes)**  Tell a story about a time when a friend supported you for being "more than the box." Use the story below if needed:

### Facilitator Story: "No Wimpin' Out!"

When I was 30, I went on a weeklong bike ride with some friends. We camped out along the way, had a lot of fun, and covered over 300 miles by the time we were finished. One night when we were sitting around the campfire, Tom, one of my friends, took out a bottle of tequila and passed it around, saying, "No wimpin' out, everyone's gotta drink." I didn't feel like drinking, so I said that I didn't want any tequila when the bottle came my way. Tom brushed off my response as if it wasn't an option: "C'mon. Don't be a wimp!" He said, "You gotta drink like everyone else!" When Tom wasn't looking, I passed the bottle to the next person. A few minutes later Tom asked me if I took a drink. Another friend of mine, Alan, jumped in. "Yeah he did," Alan said, even though he knew I passed the bottle without sipping from it. I remember being shocked, that there I was at 30 years old and I was still facing pressure to take risks to prove that I was a man. But it also felt really good that my friend Alan had spoken up to support my choice. I think that this story is a good example of how we can help our friends be more than the box.

**Outside the Box Activity**   Help the boys to identify the ways in which the behavior described in the story was outside the box. Discuss how the support of a friend allowed the facilitator to remain true to himself. Ask the boys to identify one personal characteristic or preference that they possess that is more than the box. Write down the boys' responses. Explain to the boys the point of this exercise is to help the boys find ways to support the parts of themselves that they like but that may disappear because of teasing. Ask the boys in what ways being in the group is different from the outside world.

**Treasure Hunt (50 Minutes)**   In this activity, boys must complete several physical and relational challenges in order to receive clues toward finding the "treasure."

Write down instructions for small group challenges on individual pieces of paper. Each piece of paper should contain three instructions: (1) a simple physical challenge, (2) a simple relational challenge, and (3) a clue as to where to find the next piece of paper. Here are three examples. Each example represents the three instructions written on one piece of paper.

*Example A*
1. Decide the order that each of you will read the clues and stand in a circle.
2. Say something you have learned about the boy standing to your left.
3. The next clue is hidden on the northeast corner of the school next to something orange. Run there silently now and let the next boy read the clue you find.

*Example B*
1. Order yourselves in terms of height and stand in a circle.
2. Say what your favorite activity in the boys group has been so far.
3. The next clue is hidden near the soccer goalposts. Run there silently now and let the next boy read the clue you find.

*Example C*

1. Order yourselves according to birthdates and stand in a circle.
2. Say something you appreciate about the boys born in the winter months.
3. The next clue is hidden near the flagpole. Run there silently now and let the next boy read the clue you find.

Before the group begins, hide these individual papers in different locations either inside or outside of your group space (e.g., the piece of paper hidden next to "something orange" in Example A was hidden next to a fire hydrant). Prepare the clues such that they lead the boys clearly from one hidden challenge to the next.

Relational challenges may include "appreciations" (each boy gives and receives a compliment from all other group members) and "more than the box" statements (each boy identifies a personal characteristic or interest that is not always socially acceptable for males). Preface the appreciations challenge with a statement about receiving compliments, modeling how to give them and the types of things that might be said. Sometimes boys get stuck thinking of what to say. It might be helpful to give a few seconds for the group to think before appreciating each individual. We have found it helpful to be the ones who begin the appreciations of each boy. In this way, we model for them how it is done and give them time to think of their own appreciation.

Physical challenges may include blindfolded trust walks, carrying group members some distance, boosting each other to reach high, hidden clues, and so forth. Your choices of physical challenges are flexible, but choose challenges that are quickly accomplished to preserve time for relational challenges.

**Keep in Mind...**   Boys run a great deal in this activity, and their energy is high for the mere fact of being outside. Call on boys to slow down between runs to really think about the clues of the Treasure Hunt. Remind them to take turns with one another, even though their excitement to learn about clues makes them impatient. We have found that the joyful release of running between clues actually facilitates and supports them doing the sometimes difficult relational work of giving appreciations. Their defenses seem to come down a bit after a good run. In a funny way, the appreciations almost become part of the "sport" of it.

Direct communication is particularly important during the appreciations. Ask boys to speak directly to the person being appreciated rather than casting the compliment out into space. Coach the boys to make eye contact with the person they are addressing and to say "you" rather than "he" (e.g., "You are very patient" vs. "He is very patient"). Making direct contact like this is often new for the boys and a bit uncomfortable. Be patient yet diligent about supporting this interaction. If the boys have not fully bonded by this time, this activity goes a long way toward building stronger connections.

The "more than the box" activity must be kept safe for the boys. Remind the group about being respectful and supportive. Begin by modeling how and what to share (e.g., "Okay, something that is 'outside the box' for me is that my stomach gets upset when I see violence in movies."). Boys will follow your lead. If boys continue to show confusion about what "outside the box" means, give them a few more examples: not wanting to fight, not liking sports, spending more time with girls, and so on.

**Keep in Mind...** If, for the final adventure, you are planning on going to a location other than where you have held the group, a significant amount of coordination is involved that should begin no later than this session. Hand out permission slips and information regarding the final adventure at the conclusion of this session.

Try hard to hold the final session in a setting other than where the group took place. Going on a field trip gets the boys excited and contributes to the feeling that the event is special. Getting the boys out-of-doors allows for the chance of poor weather to add extra challenge to planned activities. We have taken the boys canoeing, an activity that involves risk and cooperation, and we have hiked with the boys in a local park after dark. Sometimes going elsewhere or being outside is not possible, but the important elements of this session can be retained.

# Week 8: Trust Falling

This week, the boys face the emotionally and physically risky Trust Falling challenge, realizing a deeper level of trust in other group members.

## Session Objectives

- To strengthen group cohesion

The boys will experience stronger trust in members of the group. Because the trust falling is built up by facilitators as an activity that requires a high level of group cooperation, the trust falling should result in a heightened sense of group unity.

- To build refusal skills for the future

Boys will have the opportunity to practice declining a risk they are not comfortable with taking. There are inevitably one or two boys who do not wish to fall in the trust activity. We acknowledge those who decline, citing situations in the future where peers may be making choices with which they do not feel comfortable. We highlight how saying no can take a great deal of courage.

## What You Need

Two foam safety mats (both 2 inches thick)
Blindfolds
Paperwork for the final adventure, including a permission slip, a parent letter giving directions to the location, and a list of types of clothing needed

## What You Do

**Trust Fall Activity (60 Minutes)**  Identify a pedestal on which the fallers will stand. It should be elevated from the ground approximately 2 to 3 feet, and it should be either connected to the ground or heavy enough so that it will not move without a great deal of exerted force (e.g., a sturdy desk or table). Determine the place where the faller will stand and position safety mats on the floor, directly in front of this area (beginning 6 inches from the base of the pedestal outward). Your safety mats should be longer than your tallest person, and if you are using the 2-inch thick mats used in other activities, you should have no fewer than two stacked on top of each other.

Begin the activity by telling a story like the following:

I want you to think of a burning building for a minute. The building is tall and there are fires on the lower floors. Firefighters are holding those large, round trampoline things to catch people as they jump from the building. The toughest thing is for those people in the building to be able to trust that the firefighters will be there to catch them when they jump. We want you guys in this group to be able to count on each other in the same way. Today we are going to do a trust fall. It goes like this...

Begin this activity with clear and strict reminders about focusing on safety. As with other challenges, encourage the boys to communicate directly with one another about how goofing off jeopardizes safety. There are often boys who do not feel comfortable doing this challenge. Speak to the boys ahead of time about the difference between encouragement and pressure. We want to gently encourage the boys to take each risk, but we do not want them to feel shamed for feeling unsafe to do so. Should someone express hesitation about doing the fall, encourage the catchers to offer words of assurance, stating their resolve to keep focused and to prevent the person from getting hurt. Should the person continue to decline, offer him the opportunity to change his mind in the future.

Instruct group members to line up, shoulder to shoulder, on either side of the safety mats with an equal number of boys on each side. The two lines of boys stand facing each other. Instruct the boys from both lines to stretch their arms in front of them such that the tips of their fingers extend as far as the elbows of the boys across from them. The arms of boys facing each other should intersperse, forming a continuous bed onto which the faller will land. Boys often want to cross arms or hold each other's wrists to fortify the bed, but these variations actually weaken the bed and create an uncomfortable bumpiness or unevenness for the faller. Designate one boy to stand at the "head" of the two lines and the mats in order to support the faller's head. Coach the boys to keep their heads up and looking at the faller at all times. By slightly leaning back with their heads up, the catchers create a good size bed for the faller to fall upon.

Once the catchers are positioned, test the boys' readiness by falling onto their arms from a standing position. Once the catchers have prepared for supporting the weight of a falling body, assist the faller in climbing the pedestal. The faller should stand backward, blindfolded if he so desires, hands folded across his chest. Instruct the faller to make his body rigid in the way that was required in the Willow in the Wind activity, tensing all of the muscles in his body and falling like a board. Inform him that bending his body in the fall will make it more difficult for the boys to catch him safely. Teach the faller verbal commands to use to ensure that everyone is ready ("Ready to catch?") and to communicate when he is going to fall ("Falling!"). Teach the catchers to respond to the faller's question by saying, "Ready to catch!" and to respond to the faller's statement saying, "Fall away."

**Debriefing the Activity**   Finish the session by asking the boys about how they felt about their performance on the challenge. Did they feel safe? How did they handle the fear of falling? Was there any goofing around? Were the boys able to focus and work together enough to catch everyone? Was the faller able to remain rigid and straight, or did he fold his body, falling butt first to protect his head? Did the faller have difficulty trusting that the group would catch him? Remember to praise any of the boys who decided not to do the fall for having the courage to say no to the group. Offer examples of how saying no to the group may be very important in the future when friends are making poor or dangerous choices.

# Week 9: Talking Cards

This week, the boys review their experiences in the group, identifying areas of personal growth and considering how lessons learned will apply in the future.

## Session Objectives

- To reinforce lessons learned

The Talking Cards activity will provide qualitative indicators of the group's success with the boys. Facilitating rich discussion about lessons learned will help to sustain the impact of those lessons on the boys into the future.

- To build group cohesion

Boys will speak about the connections they have developed during their time with the group.

- To evaluate the group

Boys will complete the posttest portion of the evaluation questions.

## What You Need

Talking Cards with numerous assorted images cut from books and magazines of people, nature, and activities that represent cultural diversity

Paper and art utensils for drawing the reflection activity if you do not have the cards

Copies of the posttest evaluation

## What You Do

**Reviewing the Group (15 Minutes)**   Ask the boys to recount each week of the group, recalling the different activities and the lessons learned. Ask the boys which activities they liked the best and why. What did they feel was the most important lesson learned? How might the lesson help them with future experiences and difficult situations?

**Talking Cards Activity (35 Minutes)**   In this activity, we use a large number (100 or more) of cards with various images (cut from magazines and books, pasted to construction paper and laminated) that reflect people, places, and things. Spread the cards out on the floor face up, in front of the boys. Use the following prompt to explain the activity:

What we want you to do is this: We want you to look through all these pictures on the floor until you find three that you like. The first card we want you to pick should represent something about you before you came into this group. The second card should represent something about your experience here in the group over the past 8 weeks. The third card we want you to pick should say something about what you want to have happen in the future.

Creating your own set of cards can be a long and thoughtful process. Allow plenty of time in advance of this session to create a set should you choose to do so. However, the cards themselves are not necessary to do this activity. Instead, boys could draw three pictures, they could pick images from magazines, or they could choose three animals for representation. The important factor is that boys have three images to describe their feelings because using words alone can sometimes be difficult.

**Keep in Mind...**   This activity serves as both a reinforcement of group lessons and a qualitative evaluation of the group. Pay close attention to what boys share and consider writing their responses after the session to serve as a record of group success. If boys give little description about their chosen images or lack the words for expression, help them to fill out their ideas, checking with them about the accuracy of your interpretations.

**Planning for the Final Adventure (10 Minutes)**   Use this time to prepare boys for the last session. If your plan is to meet in a different setting, be sure that boys have accurate directions, transportation, and parent permission, if necessary. Check with boys to be sure that an adult male can accompany them and, if not, make arrangements with their parent or guardian to pair them with someone. Describe enough of your plans to build the group's excitement.

**Completing the Group Evaluation**   Give each boy a pencil and a copy of the post-test evaluation. Explain the wording of the questions to avoid any confusion. Collect all evaluations before the boys depart.

# Week 10: Found in the Woods

During this Final Adventure, boys celebrate their time in the group and say goodbye to one another. Important male figures in the lives of the boys learn about the BAM! goals and share wishes for the boys in the future.

## Session Objectives

- To explain BAM groups to significant adults males in the boys' lives

Significant males in the boys' lives will learn the BAM! philosophy to help extend the lessons for the boys. We invite fathers, older brothers, or male mentors to this final outing to support staying power for what the boys have learned in the group. By sharing with these men our concerns for boys and our philosophy about how to support them, we hope that the impact of the group will stay with the boys over time.

- To say goodbye

The boys will practice using direct communication while remaining in contact with themselves and others. We model positive endings with the boys by expressing the many feelings associated with saying goodbye and encouraging them to do the same.

## What You Need

15 to 20 candles

Headlamps, flashlights

Two volunteers to assist with logistics and hosting the adult visitors

A location for the final session that provides two distinct areas for the group: one for the group of boys and one for the group of adults; an outdoor space is preferable, but an indoor space can work

Food! Depending on the time of day and the setting, having a full meal may be appropriate or simply a fun snack

## What You Do

**Coming Together (15 Minutes)** There should be two distinct places for the boys and the men to separate initially. Boys will be dropped off at a specified location. Instruct the adults to keep heading to the final meeting spot where two volunteers await them. Allow a 15-minute window to be sure that all the boys have arrived before beginning the Challenge Medley (described on the following page).

**Preparing the Men (60 Minutes)** Meet with your volunteers before the final session and explain the BAM! group goals and activities in detail. Volunteers explain BAM! groups to the men and ask them to think of one trait or characteristic they hope for the boy they accompanied to hold onto through middle school and into adulthood. Volunteers inform the men they will be asked to share this hope publicly with the boy they accompanied in the closing circle. Allow the men plenty of unstructured time to get to know one another.

**Challenge Medley (60 Minutes)**   Create a story that frames the coming adventure and provides context for the activities you have planned. Once the full group is assembled and the men have gone to the final meeting place, share this story or something similar with the boys to begin your adventure:

> An ogre lives on this mountain, and it only comes out at night. This ogre will take any boy as victim who is isolated from the group so it is very important that you all stay together. The ogre has set traps all over this mountain to catch trespassers, and we are going to have to work well together in order to make it through those traps without alerting the ogre to our presence. It would be a shame to lose any of you on our final night together as a group.

When the story is finished, start the boys on the journey to reach the place of the final meeting. Hiking toward the final destination, require the boys to complete a few challenges that work well with the chosen environment, time of day, and group goals (e.g., blindfolded trust walks, scavenger hunts, carrying individuals for short distances, maintaining silence for short periods of time, group appreciations, etc.).

By this time, boys have a clear understanding of the purposes that the challenges serve. Spend little time processing the activities unless the boys are being really unsafe. Instead, focus on celebrating the accomplishment of each task. While moving to the next activity or destination, comment on the finer points of cooperation and communication for each challenge and/or offer feedback about glitches in the process.

**Final Circle (45 Minutes)**   When the boys reach the meeting spot, instruct them to be seated in a circle, each with a candle in front of him. Instruct the men to form a circle around the group, each standing behind the boy he accompanied. As leaders, join the circle of men wherever there is space. Begin the activity by describing the goals of BAM! groups. Then point out the positive behaviors exhibited in the group and express hope that the boys make use of the key lessons they learned. Remind the boys that certain lessons of the group may not be well received in middle school (e.g., being direct in communication of feelings), and that staying true to themselves will take courage and commitment.

Say something like, "We know that many of you will feel pressure to hide parts of yourselves as you get older in order to feel like you are becoming a man. We want the adults to go around and describe a quality of the boy you accompanied that you admire and that you hope he never loses." Next, each adult guest speaks directly to the youth he came with, describing a particular quality in the boy that he appreciates and hopes he will keep in middle school and through adulthood. If any of the men seem to struggle to find a positive quality to describe, help them with a few possible ideas. Speaking this way to boys is unfamiliar to some men. Sometimes compliments turn out to be backhanded criticisms. Tactfully assist the men without shaming their initial attempts.

Once each man has had the chance to speak, allow everyone time to socialize and eat food or snacks together, spending the last moments of the group in relaxed celebration.

To finish the group and acknowledge the end of your time together, have the boys form a final circle, putting all of their hands on top of one another in the center. Instruct boys to finish the group with the chant used to frighten away the monster of the Haunted House.

# BAM! Appendix

## BAM! Group Evaluation: Qualitative and Quantitative Methods

When we started facilitating BAM! groups 7 years ago, we also started collecting data regarding the efficacy of our approaches with boys in addressing the five goals we considered most relevant to our work with them. Stated in their most concise form, these goals are:

## BAM! Group Goals (Briefly Stated)

1. Participants will increase their awareness of the social pressures boys face and broaden their notions of what it means to be a man.
2. Participants will increase their sense of belonging, participation, and safety in a group.
3. Participants will improve their relational and communication skills.
4. Participants will expand their emotional and behavioral repertoire.
5. Participants will be able to carry the lessons from BAM! groups into other parts of their lives.

We started collecting data in the early years of our groups with more qualitative measures and have gradually added more quantitative measures. The qualitative responses have given us a vivid sense of a boy's individual experience in the group in a way that might be lost if we had only used quantitative methods to come up with numbers and percentages.

For example, in week 9 of BAM! Example we transcribed and included the rich qualitative responses from three group members—Isaiah, Sorin, and Jesus—to a question we posed to them about their overall experience in the group: Isaiah chose an image of a bunch of blueberries to "symbolize us being close as friends," Sorin chose an image of an abstract painting to represent how he felt "colorful" in the group, and Jesus chose an image of a busy crew on a yacht to represent his experience of "teamwork" in the group. The beauty and power of such words and self-selected images speak volumes to us about the power of the experience boys have in BAM! groups.

Such qualitative methods of data collection have given us richly textured and highly personal responses that have encouraged us and reminded us of why we are doing this work in the first place. The qualitative data from our groups also help us see how the boys were able to experience success at reaching some of the BAM! group goals we have just outlined. With the images they chose and the words they shared, both Isaiah and Jesus clearly spoke to their experience of "belonging, participation, and safety" in the group (as outlined in BAM! group goal 3). Sorin's chosen image and his accompanying comments about feeling "colorful" in the group not only spoke to his experience of safety with the other boys, but also to his experience of expanding his "emotional and behavioral repertoire" (as outlined in BAM! group goal 4).

We recommend that you find ways in your own work with boys to collect such qualitative data—by facilitating a similar exercise late in the group, for example, or, by frequently "checking in" with your boys about their experience in the group.

We also recommend that you use the more quantitative measures we have included to round out the data regarding how well your group members are meeting or approaching the goals of BAM! groups. We have included forms to collect data from relevant parents, teachers, and the boys themselves in order for you to have data that reflect multiple perspectives from the boy's lives (Merrell, 1999). We suggest that, during the first session of your group, you ask the boys to fill out the BAM! Group Participant Pre-Evaluation Form and that, during the last session of your group, you ask them to fill out the BAM! Group Participant Post-Evaluation Form. As the group concludes, and if you have the opportunity, we suggest that you ask the parents and the teacher of the boys to fill out the BAM! Group Adult Post-Evaluation Form. These multiple points of data collection, when looked at as a whole, will give you good information that can be used to further promote such BAM! groups in your setting. The data will also help you understand the ways you need to modify the content and process of your groups to make them more helpful and effective for the boys. Please contact us through our Web site (www.bamgroups.com) to share with us your findings.

In the next section, we share with you the linkages between the items we have included on the evaluation forms and the goals we have for the boys in our groups. You will also find the copies of the evaluation forms we have described, which you are encouraged to copy and use freely.

# Links Between BAM! Group Objectives and Evaluation Items

**BAM! Objective 1: Participants Will Increase Their Awareness of the Social Pressures Boys Face and Broaden Their Notions of What It Means to Be a Man.** Through discussion, activity, and facilitated dialogue, we expose the messages boys receive about what it means to be a man. Rather than simply stepping in line to conform to some of those unhealthful and limiting messages, we want boys to gain some ability to analyze and make choices about those messages. Boys are acutely aware of the social expectations placed on them as young men but have not had the guidance to put words to their experience. We want the boys in this group to be able to identify both positive and limiting social pressures on boys and men. Further, we want them to consider the broad range of personal qualities available to men.

### Relevant Pre- and Post-Evaluation Items
- A boy can expect to be teased if he shows weakness.
- Boys are sometimes peer-pressured into fighting.
- I think it's okay for a boy to cry.
- Boys are sometimes teased for being smart.

**BAM! Objective 2: Participants Will Increase Their Sense of Belonging, Participation, and Safety in a Group.** We are struck by boys' sense of isolation. There are few places for boys to let down their guard and relate to others authentically. Creating safe places for boys to be real is essential. In BAM! groups, boys are given this opportunity. Through activities that allow participants to identify, accept, and support similarities as well as differences among group members, boys experience themselves as unique but not alone. As a result, boys in our groups create and strengthen friendships within the group.

### Relevant Pre- and Post-Evaluation Items
- I belong to a group of friends in which my ideas are respected.
- I belong to a group of friends in which it is okay to be myself.
- I feel lonely.
- I feel like I don't have any friends.

**BAM! Objective 3: Participants Will Improve Their Relational and Communication Skills.** Many of the problems boys face stem from the difficulties they have in skillfully relating to others. BAM! group leaders choreograph experiences in which participants can be honest, respectful, and direct in their communication with both the adults and the boys in the group. We recognize when boys actively listen to and empathize with others in the group. Activities encourage the boys to work cooperatively with others in the group.

### Relevant Pre- and Post-Evaluation Items
- It is difficult for me to talk about how I am feeling.
- I can speak up for myself when someone is pressuring me.
- I care about how others feel.
- I am good at working in a group.

**BAM! Objective 4: Participants Will Expand Their Emotional and Behavioral Repertoire.** We want boys to become more emotionally fluent. In BAM! groups, boys are coached to identify and express a broad range of emotions. At the same time, many boys have difficulties due to impulsive behavior and unchecked anger. Through initiatives, guided conversation, and direct instruction, boys are taught to more skillfully manage and regulate emotions and behaviors like impulsivity, aggression, and anger.

### Relevant Pre- and Post-Evaluation Items
- I am good at thinking before I act.
- I am good at knowing when I am mad and can talk to others about it.
- I am good at controlling my feelings when I need to.

**BAM! Objective 5: Participants Will be Able to Carry the Lessons from BAM! Groups Into Other Parts of Their Lives.** We want the lessons and experiences boys gain from these groups to make a difference in their lives now and in the future. The social pressures placed on boys are enormous. We work with them to increase their ability to use refusal skills, make healthy decisions, and choose good friends so that they have support to be healthy young men. Lastly, we assist boys to identify personal strengths that they can carry outside the group.

### Relevant Post-Evaluation Items
- I learned things in this group that will help me in middle school.
- I have used things that I learned in this group outside of this group.
- I sometimes think about our group discussions outside of our group sessions.
- I have talked to other people in my life about this group.
- I have made friendships in the group.

# BAM! Group Participant Pre-Evaluation Form

*For each item below, please place a check under the response that fits best for you. Please fill this form out during the first session of the BAM! group.*

|  |  | Strongly Agree | Agree | Don't Know | Disagree | Strongly Disagree |
|---|---|---|---|---|---|---|
| 1. | Boys are sometimes teased for being smart. |  |  |  |  |  |
| 2. | I belong to a group of friends in which it is okay for me to be myself. |  |  |  |  |  |
| 3. | I can speak up for myself when someone is pressuring me. |  |  |  |  |  |
| 4. | It is difficult for me to talk about how I am feeling. |  |  |  |  |  |
| 5. | I am good at working in a group. |  |  |  |  |  |
| 6. | Boys are sometimes peer-pressured into fighting. |  |  |  |  |  |
| 7. | I belong to a group of friends in which my ideas are respected. |  |  |  |  |  |
| 8. | I am good at thinking before I act. |  |  |  |  |  |
| 9. | I am good at controlling my feelings when I need to. |  |  |  |  |  |
| 10. | I feel lonely. |  |  |  |  |  |
| 11. | I feel like I don't have any friends. |  |  |  |  |  |
| 12. | A boy can expect to be teased if he shows weakness. |  |  |  |  |  |
| 13. | I am good at knowing when I am mad and can talk to others about it. |  |  |  |  |  |
| 14. | I think that it is okay for a boy to cry. |  |  |  |  |  |
| 15. | I care about how others feel. |  |  |  |  |  |

# BAM! Group Participant Post-Evaluation Form (Part 1)

*Please check the box that best fits your response for each item below. Please fill this form out during the last session of the BAM! group.*

| | | Strongly Agree | Agree | Don't Know | Disagree | Strongly Disagree |
|---|---|---|---|---|---|---|
| 1. | Boys are sometimes teased for being smart. | | | | | |
| 2. | I belong to a group of friends in which it is okay for me to be myself. | | | | | |
| 3. | I can speak up for myself when someone is pressuring me. | | | | | |
| 4. | It is difficult for me to talk about how I am feeling. | | | | | |
| 5. | I am good at working in a group. | | | | | |
| 6. | Boys are sometimes peer-pressured into fighting. | | | | | |
| 7. | I belong to a group of friends in which my ideas are respected. | | | | | |
| 8. | I am good at thinking before I act. | | | | | |
| 9. | I am good at controlling my feelings when I need to. | | | | | |
| 10. | I feel lonely. | | | | | |
| 11. | I feel like I don't have any friends. | | | | | |
| 12. | A boy can expect to be teased if he shows weakness. | | | | | |
| 13. | I am good at knowing when I am mad and can talk to others about it. | | | | | |
| 14. | I think that it is okay for a boy to cry. | | | | | |
| 15. | I care about how others feel. | | | | | |
| 16. | I learned things in this group that will help me in middle school. | | | | | |
| 17. | I have used things that I learned in this group outside of this group. | | | | | |
| 18. | I think about our group discussions outside of our group sessions. | | | | | |
| 19. | I have talked to other people in my life about this group. | | | | | |
| 20. | I have made friends in the group. | | | | | |

# BAM! Group Participant Post-Evaluation Form (Part 2)

*During the last session of the BAM! group, please write your responses to the following prompts in the spaces below.*

Some of my favorite things in this group were:

Some things I wanted to do more in the group were:

Some things I wanted to do less of in this group were:

Some important things I learned in the group are:

# BAM! Group Adult Post-Evaluation Form

*After the last session of the BAM! group, please check the box that best fits your response for items 1 to 5 below and add your comments to the prompts in items 6 to 10. Thank you!*

|   |   | Strongly Agree | Agree | Don't Know | Disagree | Strongly Disagree |
|---|---|---|---|---|---|---|
| 1. | His experience in this group met my expectations. | | | | | |
| 2. | He has talked to me and other people in his life about this group. | | | | | |
| 3. | He has made friends in the group. | | | | | |
| 4. | He has used things that he learned in this group outside of the group. | | | | | |
| 5. | I would recommend this group to others. | | | | | |

6. The reasons I wanted him to be in this group were:

7. The ways I have seen this group have an effect on him are:

8. The things I liked about this group are:

9. The things I would suggest changing about this group are:

10. Please add additional comments, if any, on the back of this sheet.

## Sample Permission Form

### Boys Advocacy and Mentoring (BAM!)
### Boys Lunch Groups

*Why?*

We are concerned that too often boys in our society learn to interact with one another in ways that are hurtful, involve put-downs, and generally do not foster safe and supportive friendships. In contrast, we want to create an environment where boys can feel safer with and more supported by one another, with less of a need to act aggressively or defensively. We want the boys in the Boys Lunch Group to use their naturally buoyant and expressive energies in mutually supportive ways in order to experience a positive sense of belonging, safety, and involvement in their classrooms, in their school, and in their community.

*How?*

We start off our weekly, lunchtime group meetings stressing the importance of rules like "no put-downs" and "no interrupting" in order to develop positive and supportive ways of interacting with one another. We use trust-building activities, games, and discussions to help the boys to experience what it is like to count on and trust one another. We also work to create an atmosphere of fun and friendship for the boys to be part of each week.

For one of our last sessions, we like to take boys out on a "Saturday Adventure" that is challenging for the boys, but that is also safe and fun. During this outing they get to practice their cooperation and communication skills.

*Who?*

This winter the group will be led by _____. Boys are chosen for the group by parent, teacher, and self-nomination.

*When?*

The group will meet (when, where) _____.

If you are interested in this opportunity for your student, please sign below to indicate your permission. If you have any questions about the group, please contact _____.

_____        _____        _____
Student Name            Parent/Guardian Signature            Date
Telephone Number: (h)                              (w)

## Additional Activities and Discussion Topics

In this section, we offer additional activities, sorted by BAM! objectives.

*BAM! Objective #1: Helping participants increase their awareness of the social pressures boys face and broaden their notions of what it means to be a man.*

### Deconstruct Manliness Messages

In recent years we have done a better job of helping young women to critique media messages about women. We have not done as well at helping boys to deconstruct media messages about men. You can use ads from print or television to discuss the messages they communicate about what it means to be a man. One beer ad we saw recently used the tagline, "Share beer, not feelings." Discuss the message this sends boys about what it means to be a man. Consider how these messages affect boys and men.

### Act Like a Man Box

This activity, which we used in weeks 5 and 6, can be altered in many ways depending on the age group. We first saw this activity in the book *Helping Teens Stop Violence* by Creighton and Kivel (1992) published by Hunter House. Start with a list of male qualities promoted by popular culture. In other words, "According to music television, sports and video games, a man is supposed to be. . . . " You should get responses like a man is supposed to be unemotional, tough, athletic, buff, and so forth. Record that list on a piece of flipchart paper. Then draw a box around that list. Next ask, "What if there is a boy who is different than this box?"—for example, a boy who plays with girls, doesn't like sports, or is seen crying. "What are the names he is likely to be called?" You will get words like "fag, girl, wuss, sissy."

Next, ask what effect these names have on the boy who is called them. People will say things like, "He feels bad, or he may withdraw, or he gets mad." It is important to demonstrate the social pressure that boys face that leads them to conform to the box, so follow up with a question like, "Then what happens?" Ultimately, we want to illustrate that boys conform to the box out of fear of being shamed by being thought of as soft, feminine, or having girl-like qualities. From here the discussion could go many places, including ways that we are more than the box and ways that we support other boys to be more than the box.

### Take a Stand

This is a good activity to begin to flush out assumptions about being a boy. It can be used as an introduction to the Act Like a Man Box as it tends to elicit some of the ideas that get discussed in Act Like a Man. To do this activity, place a sign that says "Agree" on one wall and a sign that says "Disagree" on an opposite wall. Have the boys stand in the middle of the room and read one of the following sentences, then have the boys take a stand to agree or disagree with the statement. Before you read any sentences, encourage the boys to think on their own rather than being swayed by their peers.

1. Boys are just born more violent than girls.
2. Girls are more likely to notice boys who goof around than those who get good grades.
3. It is more acceptable for boys to get mad than to cry.
4. Boys who are good fighters get more respect than those who work to resolve conflicts.
5. Children need mothers at home more than they need their fathers.

## A Man You Look Up To

These are good follow-up discussions for the Act Like a Man Box:

- Name a man you look up to and describe why.
- In what ways is this man in the box?
- In what ways is this man more than the box?

## Father Conversations

Regardless of a father's level of involvement in his son's life, his impact on his son is very great. Boys have strong feelings about their fathers, whether or not they are present. It is fruitful to find ways to talk about dads and to point out similarities and differences among group members. You may ask:

- What are some things you admire about your dad?
- What do you like least about your dad?
- What are the characteristics of a good father?
- From your perspective, what are some dos and don'ts of fatherhood?

*BAM! Objective #2: Additional activities to help participants increase their sense of belonging, participation, and safety in a group.*

## Silent Circle Dash

This is a good energizer that creates focus and contact without using words. Have everyone stand in a circle around one person who's standing in the middle. The object of the game is for any two people in the circle to silently signal each other and switch places. A player can't move on his own. He must make visual contact with someone and signal a sort of agreement. This demands some connection between players. While the players on the outside are trading places, the person in the middle tries to take one of the vacated spots. The person left without a spot in the circle takes the spot in the middle for the next round. This is a silent game.

## Monster Cards

This activity uses Yu-Gi-Oh! or other such trading cards to elicit a conversation about feelings. Boys are asked to draw a monster card that reflects a particular feeling, such as "scary," and name their monster. Examples may be "lost in a mall monster" or getting "picked on by a bully monster." After they draw their cards, boys are asked to describe why their card is the scariest (or saddest or most embarrassing, etc.). This works because it allows indirect expression of an emotional experience using art and also plays into boys' propensity for competition.

*BAM! Objective #4: Helping participants expand emotional and behavioral repertoire.*

## Defining Impulsivity

Many boys get into trouble because of impulsive behavior. Some have even been called impulsive but have never been told what this means. We break it down like this:

1. Impulsive means to *feel~act~think*
2. Self-control means to *feel~calm~think~act*

We ask the boys to describe an example of a time when they acted impulsively and a time when they showed self-control. We then analyze their examples according to our definition of impulsivity or self-control. Often, boys who have been told they are impulsive have a difficult time identifying examples of times when they exercised self-control. They often need help coming up with examples. For these boys it is important that we help them to change their identity to include the ability for self-control. We work to help them find examples of self-control, coach parents to notice these examples, and help the boy himself to recognize that this behavior is within his repertoire.

## Calming, Slowing Down

There are many ways to talk to boys about calming. Practicing deep breathing and variations on breathing exercises can be very effective. First, discuss the autonomic nervous system's response to stress and how breathing becomes shorter and more rapid under stress. Also discuss that longer, slower breaths help the body and mind to calm.

Then practice various breathing exercises. We have the boys place a hand on their abdomen and a hand on their chest to feel their breath. Then we encourage them to take full breaths so that they can experience their abdomen *and* chest expanding. We coach them to expand their abdomen then their chest and to release their chest then their abdomen. We breathe as a group like this for five rounds and discuss how it affects them.

We sometimes extend this to encourage focused breathing and deeper relaxation. We count and have participants inhale and exhale with our count. For example, "Inhale 2-3-4, exhale 2-3-4, inhale 2-3-4-5-6-7-8, exhale 2-3-4-5-

6-7-8. . . . " We usually count to 4 then 8 then 10 then 12 then 10 then 8 then 4, ending with some quiet moments of them breathing on their own. We debrief with a discussion of how this changed their state of mind.

## Being Assertive Is HARD

Boys often need help being more assertive. As in the Defining Impulsivity activity listed on the previous page, a lot can be gained by defining the terms *passive*, *assertive*, and *aggressive*. We use the acronym HARD (honest, appropriate, respectful, direct).

1. Assertive communication is *honest, appropriate, respectful,* and *direct*.
2. Passive communication is *appropriate* and *respectful.*
3. Assertive communication is *honest* and *direct*.

We let the boys know that they are most likely to get their needs met without negative consequences when they act assertively. We share examples of different situations with friends or adults and have the boys analyze whether the response is passive, aggressive, or assertive. We then can use this model to examine interactions within the group.

# References

Alexandera, G. M. (2002). Sex differences in response to children's toys in nonhuman primates (Cercopithecus aethiops sabaeus). *Evolution and Human Behavior, 23,* 467–479.

Anderson, R. N., & Smith, B. L. (2003). Deaths: Leading causes for 2001. *National Vital Statistics Report, 52,* 1–52.

Angelou, M. (1990). *I shall not be moved.* New York: Random House.

Bandura, R. A. (1986). *Social foundations of thought and action: A social cognitive theory.* Englewood Cliffs, NJ: Prentice Hall.

Barkley, R. A. (1998). *Attention-deficit hyperactivity disorder: A handbook for diagnosis and treatment.* New York: Guildford Press.

Baron-Cohen, S. (2003). *The essential difference: The truth about the male and female brain.* New York: Basic Books.

Baron-Cohen S., Richler, J., Bisarya, D., et al. (2003). The systemizing quotient: an investigation of adults with Asperger syndrome or high functioning autism, and normal sex differences. Special Issue on Autism, Mind and Brain. *Philosophical Transactions of the Royal Society B, 358,* 361–740.

Benson, P. L., Roehlkepartain, J. L., & Leffert, N. (1997). *Starting out right: Developmental assets for children.* Minneapolis, MN: Search Institute.

Berenbaum, S. A. (2000). Psychological outcome in congenital adrenal hyperplasia. In B. Stabler & B. B. Bercy (Eds.), *Therapeutic outcome of endocrine disorders: Efficacy, innovation, and quality of life* (pp. 186–199). New York: Springer.

Berenbaum, S. A., & Resnick, S. M. (1997). Early androgen effects on aggression in children and adults with congenital adrenal hyperplasia. *Psychoneuroendocrinology, 22,* 505–515.

Bowlby, J. (1988). *A secure base.* New York: Basic Books.

Brown, D. E. (1991). *Human universals.* New York: McGraw-Hill.

Bruner, J. (1990). *Acts of meaning.* Cambridge, MA: Harvard University Press.

Buhrmester, D. (1996). Need fulfillment, interpersonal competence and the developmental contexts of early adolescent friendship. In W. M. Bukowski, A.F. Newcomb, & W. W. Hartup (Eds.), *The company they keep: Friendship in childhood and adolescence* (pp. 158–185). New York: Cambridge University Press.

Burr, J. E., Ostrov, J. M., and Jansen, E. A. (2005). Relational aggression and friendship during early childhood: "I won't be your friend!" *Early Education & Development, 16,* 161–185.

Butler, S., & Rohnke, K. (1995). *Quicksilver: Adventure games, initiative problems, trust activities and a guide to effective leadership.* Dubuque, IA: Kendall/Hunt Publishing Company.

Camarena, P. M., Sarigiani, P. A., & Petersen, A. C. (1990). Gender-specific pathways to intimacy in early adolescence. *Journal of Youth and Adolescence, 19,* 19–32.

Castellanos, F. X., Lee, P. P., and Sharp, W. (2002). Developmental trajectories of brain volume abnormalities in children and adolescents with attention-deficit/hyperactivity disorder. *Journal of the American Medical Association, 288,* 1740–1748.

Connellan, J. (2001). Sex differences in human neonatal social perception. *Infant Brain and Development, 23,* 113–118.

Creighton, A., & Kivel, P. (1992). *Helping teens stop violence.* Alameda, CA: Hunter House.

Crick, N. R. (1996). The role of overt aggression, relational aggression, and prosocial behavior in the prediction of children's future social adjustment. *Child Development, 67,* 2317–2327.

Crick, N. R., & Grotpeter, J. K. (1995). Relational aggression, gender, and social-psychological adjustment. *Child Development, 66,* 710–722.

Diller, L. (1999). *Running on Ritalin.* New York: Bantam.

Eaton, W. O., & Enns, L. R. (1986). Sex differences in human motor activity level. *Psychological Bulletin, 100,* 19–28.

Hall, J. A. (1984). *Nonverbal sex differences: communication accuracy and expressive style.* Baltimore: The Johns Hopkins University Press.

Hall, J. A., Carter, J. D., & Horgan, T. G. (2000). Gender differences in nonverbal communication of emotion. In A. H. Fischer (Ed.), *Gender and emotion: Social psychological perspectives* (pp. 97–117). Cambridge, UK: Cambridge University Press.

Halpern, D. (2005). Sex, brains, & hands: Gender differences in cognitive abilities. *Skeptic, 2,* 96–103.

Hankin, B. L., & Abramson L. Y. (1999) Development of gender differences in depression: Description and possible explanations. *Annals of Medicine, 31,* 372–379.

Heesacker, M., Wester, S. R., Vogel, D. L., et al. (1999). Gender-based emotional stereotyping. *Journal of Counseling Psychology, 46,* 483–495.

Holmgren, D. (2007). The essence of permaculture. Available at: http://www.holmgren.com.au/html/Writings/essence.htmlFootnotes

Institute of Medicine. (2001). *Exploring the biological contributions to human health: Does sex matter?* Washington, DC: National Academy Press.

Junaid, K. A., & Fellowes, S. (2006). Gender differences in the attainment of motor skills on the Movement Assessment Battery for children. *Physical & Occupational Therapy in Pediatrics, 26,* 5–11.

Kimura, D. (1995). Estrogen replacement therapy may protect against intellectual decline in postmenopausal women. *Hormones and Behavior, 29,* 312–321.

Kindlon, D., Thompson, M., & Barker, T. (2000). *Raising Cain: Protecting the emotional life of boys.* New York: Ballantine.

Kiselica, M. S. (2001). A male-friendly therapeutic process with school-age boys. In G. R. Brooks & G. E. Good (Eds.), *The new handbook of psychotherapy and counseling with men* (vol. 1, pp. 41–58). San Francisco: Jossey-Bass.

Kiselica, M. S. (2003). Transforming psychotherapy in order to succeed with adolescent boys: Male-friendly practices. *JCLP/In Session, 59,* 1225–1236.

Kiselica, M. S., & O'Brien, S. (2001). Are attachment disorders and alexithymia characteristic of males? In M. S. Kiselica (Chair), *Are males really emotional mummies: What do the data indicate?* Symposium at the 109th Annual Convention of the American Psychological Association, San Francisco, CA.

Kottler, J. A. (2001). *Learning group leadership: An experiential approach.* Boston: Allyn & Bacon.

Knickmeyer, R. S., & Wheelwright, S. (2005). Gender-typed play and amniotic testosterone. *Developmental Psychology, 41,* 517–528.

Kraemer, S. (2000). The fragile male. *British Medical Journal, 321,* 1609–1612.

Kuhlmann, S. L., & Wolf, O. (2005). Cortisol and memory retrieval in women: Influence of menstrual cycle and oral contraceptives. *Psychopharmacology (Berlin), 183,* 65–71.

LaFrance, M., & Hecht, M. A. (2000). Gender and smiling: A meta-analysis of sex differences in smiling. In A. H. Fischer (Ed.), *Gender and emotion* (pp. 118–142). Cambridge, UK: Cambridge University Press.

Lutchmaya, S., & Baron-Cohen, S. (2002). Human sex differences in social and non-social looking preferences at twelve months of age. *Infant Behavior and Development, 25,* 319–325.

Lutchmaya, S., Baron-Cohen, S., & Raggat, P. (2002a). Foetal testosterone and vocabulary size in 18- and 24-month-old infants. *Infant Behavior and Development, 24,* 418–424.

Lutchmaya, S., Baron-Cohen, S., & Raggat, P. (2002b). Foetal testosterone and eye contact at twelve months. *Infant Behavior and Development, 25,* 327–335.

Maccoby, E. E. (1998). *The two sexes: Growing up apart, coming together.* Cambridge, MA: Harvard University Press.

Manstead, A. S. (1992). Gender differences in emotion. In A. Gale & M. Eysenck (Eds.), *Handbook of individual differences: Biological perspectives* (pp. 355–387). New York: Wiley.

McClure, E.B. (2000). A meta-analytic review of sex differences in facial expression processing and their development in infants, children, and adolescents. *Psychological Bulletin,* 126 (3): 424–453.

McNelles, L., & Connolly, J. (1999). Intimacy between adolescent friends: Age and gender differences in intimate affect and intimate behaviors. *Journal of Research on Adolescence, 9,* 143–159.

Merrell, K. W. (1999). *Behavioral, social and emotional assessment of children and adolescents* (2nd ed.). Mahwah, NJ: Lawrence Erlbaum Associates.

Merrell, K. W., & Popinga, M. R. (1994). Parent-teacher concordance and gender differences in behavioral ratings of social skills and social-emotional problems of primary-age children with disabilities. *Diagnostique, 19,* 1–14.

Mortola, P. (2003). Talking cards. In H. G. Kaduson, & C. E. Schaefer (Eds.), *101 Favorite play therapy techniques* (vol. 3, pp. 286–289). Northvale, NJ: Jason Aronson, Inc.

Mortola, P. (2006). *Windowframes: Learning the art of gestalt play therapy the Oaklander way.* Hillsdale, NJ: Gestalt Press/Analytic Press.

Munroe, R. L., Hulefeld, R., Rodgers, J., Tomeo, D. L., & Yamazaki, S. K. (2000). Aggression among children in four cultures. *Cross Cultural Research, 34,* 3–25.

National Center for Education Statistics. (2005). *Gender differences in participation and completion of undergraduate education and how they have changed over time.* Available at: http://nces.ed.gov/pubsearch/pubsinfo.asp?pubid=2005169

Northeastern Wisconsin In-School Telecommunications. *What's up with middle school guys?* [Video documentary]. (Available from NEWIST/CESA 7 Video Store, 2420 Nicolet Drive, IS 1040, Green Bay, WI 54311)

Oaklander, V. (1978). *Windows to our children: A gestalt therapy approach to children and adolescents.* Highland, NY: The Gestalt Journal.

Orozco, S., & Ehlers, C. L. (1998). Gender differences in electrophysiological responses to facial stimuli. *Biological Psychiatry, 15,* 281–289.

Patterson, F. G. P., Holts, C., & Saphire, L. (1991). Cyclic changes in hormonal, physical, behavioral, and linguistic measures in female lowland gorilla. *American Journal of Primatology, 24,* 181–194.

Perls, F., Hefferline, R., & Goodman, P. (1951). *Gestalt therapy: Excitement and growth in the human personality.* New York: Dell Publishing.

Piaget, J. (1962). *Play, dreams and imitation in childhood.* New York: W. W. Norton.

Pollack, W. (1998). *Real boys.* New York: Random House.

Pope, H. G., Jr., Olivardia, R., Gruber, A., & Borowiecki, J. (1999). Evolving ideals of male body image as seen through action toys. *International Journal of Eating Disorders, 26,* 65–72.

Resnick, M. D. (1997). Protecting adolescents from harm. Findings from the National Longitudinal Study on Adolescent Health. *Journal of the American Medical Association, 278,* 823.

Reynolds, C. R., & Kamphaus, R. W. (1992). *Behavior assessment system for children: Manual.* Circle Pines, MN: American Guidance.

Siegel, D. (1999). *The developing mind.* New York: Guilford.

Soifer, D. (2002). *Special education reform 2002: Where to begin?* Arlington, VA: Lexington Institute.

Tannen, D. (1990). *You just don't understand.* New York: Morrow.

Tannen, D. (1994). *Gender and discourse.* New York: Oxford University Press.

Tomkins, S. S. (1962). *Affect imagery consciousness: The positive affects* (vol. 1). New York: Springer.

Vaishnav, A., & Dedman, B. (2002, July 8). Special ed gender gap stirs worry. *Boston Globe.* Retrieved July 8, 2002, from http://www.boston.com

Vygotsky, L. S. (1962, 1934). *Thought and language.* Cambridge, MA: MIT Press.

Way, N., & Chu, J. Y. (Eds.). (2004). *Adolescent boys: Exploring diverse cultures of boyhood.* New York: New York University Press.

Wester, S. R., Vogel, D. L., Pressly, P. K., & Heesacker, M. (2002). Sex differences in emotion: A critical review of the literature and implications for counseling psychology. *The Counseling Psychologist, 30,* 629–651.

Wheeler, G. (1991). *Gestalt reconsidered: A new approach to contact and resistance.* New York: Gardner Press.

Woods, E. (1996). Associations of nonverbal decoding ability with indices of person-centered communicative ability. *Communication Reports, 9,* 13–22.

Wright, R. (1994). *The moral animal: Why we are the way we are: The new science of evolutionary psychology.* New York: Random House.

# Index

challenges faced by, 1–2, 14
contact style of, 9–12
expectations about, 49–51
recruiting for group, 72
similarities between girls and, 13–14
social influences on, 5–8
strengths of, 13–16
successful engagement with, 3–4

## C

Calming, 128–129
Cars, 11
Challenge activities, 39–41, 47
Closing adventure, 65–67, 83–88
Comforts, 75
Communication skills
    gender and, 10–11
    improving, 19–20
Community receptivity, 69–70
Congenital adrenal hyperplasia (CAH),
        11–12
Contact
    approaches to better, 17–18
    authentic, 55
    Gestalt model of, 3–4
    helping boys make better, 19–20
    necessity of good, 3–4
    through physical challenges, 26–28
    through strategic storytelling, 23–25
Contact style
    of boys, 9–12
    strengths of boys', 13–16
Counseling, traditional, 8
Cultural messages, about masculinity, 5–8

## D

Data collection, 69–70, 117–118
Defense mechanisms, 5–6
Difficult behavior, 78–79
Diller, Lawrence, 2
Directness, 17–18
Disclosure, 77–78
Drop outs, 2
Drug abuse, 6
Dysfunctional beliefs, about masculinity,
        5–8

## E

Electric Fence activity, 32–33, 86–87
Emotional disturbances, 2
Emotions
    bottling up, 43
    censoring of, due to social influences, 5
    disconnection with, 3
    expanding repertoire of, 20
    expressing, 76
    indirect expression of, 17
    lack of ownership of, 5–6
    losing touch with, 1
    misreading of boys', 7
    processing of, by boys, 7
    range of, 36
    similarities among, 13
    of young boys, 1
Empathy, 5–6, 14
Estrogen, 11
Evaluation methods, 117–118
Evolution, 11
Expectations, 49–51

## F

Facial expressions, 10, 13
Facilitator stories, 23–25, 30–33, 35–36,
        42–43, 45–46, 49, 52
Family situations, 42–44
Father conversations, 127
Feelings, *see* Emotions
Females; *see also* Girls
    as group leaders, 79–81
    preference of, for faces, 10
Found in the Woods activity, 65–67,
        113–115
Friendships, 5, 15
Fun, 75

## G

Gender roles, flexibility of, 9
Gestalt perspective, 3–4
Girls
    aggression by, 14
    challenges faced by, 14
    language skills of, 10–11
    processing of emotions by, 7
    similarities between boys and, 13–14

# Notes